THE IMAGE OF LEADERSHIP IN HEALTH CARE

Special Edition, 10th Anniversary

THE IMAGE OF LEADERSHIP IN HEALTH CARE

*How Leaders in Health Care Package Themselves
to Stand Out for All the Right Reasons*

by
Sylvie di Giusto

Copyright © 2024 Sylvie di Giusto LLC
All rights reserved

No part of this book may be reproduced in any form or by any electronic or mechanical means including information storage and retrieval systems, without permission in writing from the author. The only exception is by a reviewer, who may quote short excerpts in a published review.

The information presented herein represents the views of the author as of the date of publication. This book is presented for informational purposes only. Due to the rate at which conditions change, the author reserves the right to alter and update her opinions at any time. While every attempt has been made to verify the information in this book, the author does not assume any responsibility for errors, inaccuracies, or omissions.

ISBN: 978-8-9901927-0-6

To the silent warriors and everyday champions,
whose dedication, spirit, and resilience
speak louder than words ever could.

Contents

About This Special Edition 9
Foreword by Dr. Arlan Fuhr 11
Introduction 15
Chapter 1: Seven Seconds 20
    The Cost of a Poor Professional Imprint 27
Chapter 2: Your Professional Imprint 32
    The Science of First Impressions 37
    The Sustained Imprint 40
    The Invisible Filters of Perception 45
    Stand Out for the Right Reasons 50
    When Details Speak Loudest 53
    The ABCDEs of Your Professional Imprint 56
    Internal and External Consistency 61
Chapter 3: Leaders Look Confident 66
    Leaders Are Confident about Their Body 68
    Leaders Are Confident about Their Age 72
    Leaders Are Confident about Their Gender 74
    Leaders Are Confident about Their Style 77
Chapter 4: Leaders Look Authentic 80
    Keywords Are the Keys to Authenticity 82
    The Explorer: Approachable and Relaxed 86
    The Traditionalist: Trustworthy and Reliable 87
    The Cosmopolitan: Sophisticated and Eloquent 88
    The Caregiver: Supportive and Nurturing 90
    The Avant-Garde: Individualistic and Creative 91
    The Glamorous: Magnetic and Extravagant 93
    The Dramatic: Strong and Fearless 94

Chapter 5: Leaders Look Professional 98
From Scrubs to Suits: The Spectrum of Health Care Attire 101
Uniforms: Traditional Signatures of Health Care Expertise 103
Beyond Uniforms: Weaving Individuality into Your Attire 104
High-Stakes Style: Dressing for Health Care's Elite Roles 106
Dressing beyond the Code: Situational Awareness 108

Chapter 6: Leaders Look Respectful 112
It's a Sign of Self-Respect 113
It Shows That You Respect Others 114

Chapter 7: Leaders Look Controlled 118
Self-Awareness and Self-Reflection 120
Self-Care and Self-Discipline 121
Self-Improvement and Self-Promotion 123
Keeping Control in the Midst of Chaos 124
Be Prepared for the Predictable and the Unpredictable 125
It's Not Only about Clothes 126

Chapter 8: Leadership in a Digital Landscape 132
KNOW: Assessing the Scope of Your e-Shadow 134
REPAIR: Correcting Your Cyber Image 137
OWN: Claiming Your Virtual Real Estate 138
CONTROL: Commanding Your Digital Boundaries 140
MONITOR: Persistent Surveillance of Your Online Self 141

Chapter 9: Leaders Lead by Example 144
The Leader's Challenge: It's Not You, It's Someone Else 147

Chapter 10: Moving Forward 158

Acknowledgments 163

About the Author 164

Perception Audit 165

Your Voice and Our Collective Reach 166

About This Special Edition

Ten years ago, I released *The Image of Leadership*, not fully grasping the impact it would have on my own career trajectory. At that time, I remember feeling a mix of excitement and nervousness. After all, releasing a book into the world is no small feat. Just a few weeks before I hit that "Publish" button, Mark Sanborn, a titan of leadership thought and Hall of Fame speaker himself, gave me a piece of advice that has stayed with me: "Nobody cares about your first book, but everybody cares that you have a first book." You know, in the speaking world, a book is an entry point, a business card, a conversation starter—a testament to your thoughts and expertise.

That book did indeed open doors and sparked conversations, fulfilling its role perfectly—and much more. But Mark wasn't finished after his original words. He turned around and, while walking off, threw a greater challenge my way: "But you really must write a good second book, Sylvie." So consider this edition my "second good book," the refined version of my initial offering.

You see, a lot has changed in ten years. The digital landscape has evolved rapidly, social media has reshaped our connections, casual work attire has become more accepted, and diversity and inclusion have taken center stage. And we can't forget the profound impact of the pandemic. It was clear that *The Image of Leadership* needed more than just a touch-up—it needed a transformation.

The book needed a comprehensive renewal to stay relevant in a world that has fundamentally shifted. And so I embarked on a journey of complete revision rather than mere superficial changes. This wasn't just about updating; it was about reimagining and realigning the book with the times we live in.

In this process, I made a conscious decision to dedicate these special editions to the incredible individuals I've met and spoken to over the years. You know, as a keynote speaker, the exchange is a two-way street. For every insight I've offered from the stage, I've received an equal measure of wisdom from my audiences. The specific challenges they've shared, the questions they've asked, and the stories they've told have enriched my understanding and approach to leadership.

I'm immensely thankful for this reciprocal learning. It's this exchange that has breathed new life into *The Image of Leadership*, transforming it into a special edition that reflects not just my voice but also the collective voice of the many dedicated professionals in health care I've had the honor to engage with.

This special edition is dedicated to those health care professionals. It's tailored to address the unique challenges and triumphs you face daily. It's more than just an update; it's a recommitment to the principles of leadership tailored to the nuances of your world—where stakes are high and the demands are unlike those of any other profession.

Here's to you, the health care leaders, who embody resilience and dedication every day. This book is for you—the ethical, the compassionate, the driven. It's a thank-you for your service and a tool to aid your journey forward.

Consider this book the "second" that Mark Sanborn urged me to perfect—a version refined by experience and honed by the passage of time. It's a handbook for the present, a road map for the future, and a testament to the enduring power of a leader's image in the high-stakes world of health care.

May this special edition serve you as a beacon through the ever-changing landscape of leadership in health care, inspiring you to continue making impactful decisions with confidence, care, and authority.

Foreword
by Dr. Arlan Fuhr

I have been a health care professional for 60 years. I imagine what my journey as a seasoned doctor of chiropractic would have been like had I had access to *The Image of Leadership in Health Care* back then. I would not have struggled to find myself the way that I did when I first started practicing.

A bit about me will help guide the reader into understanding why what I say has merit. I am the cofounder and chairman of Activator Methods International and the coinventor of the Activator Adjusting Instrument and the Activator Methods Chiropractic Technique (AMCT), which was established in 1967. It is the world's most accepted instrument adjusting chiropractic technique, and its protocol is taught in nearly all chiropractic colleges in the United States and abroad. It is a non-force, gentle way to adjust a patient.

I am an alumnus of Logan University in Chesterfield, Missouri, a suburb of St. Louis, but I was raised in a small farming community in rural Minnesota, where the dress of the day was a pair of Levi's and a T-shirt. Following graduation, I spent two years in the United States Navy, and shortly thereafter I found myself back in my hometown.

I was a 24-year-old veteran with no money and no place to practice. My field doctor in the military, Dr. W. C. Lee, suggested I start practicing with him until I could decide where I wanted to work. Dr. Lee sat me down and explained to me the rules of dress for a doctor. He said, in practice, I was to present myself in a button-down white shirt, tie, and white clinic jacket that he had provided me, along with a name tag that read, "Dr. A. W. Fuhr."

This was my first lesson on looking like a doctor. I laughed and cried as I read parts of this book, thinking how it could have made my journey so much easier had I had access to its pearls so long ago.

As I read Sylvie's book, I was blown away by the fact that a person, a patient, made up their mind about their doctor, those like me, in seven seconds. Sylvie calls it the "seven-second rule." I was lucky that Dr. Lee took the time to sit me down and teach me how to dress the part of a doctor. He also suggested I buy a pair of glasses, even though I did not need them to see. He said it would make me look older.

This book discusses how two competent doctors impressed or unimpressed the interviewer for a very important job. My wife has a saying, "Wear the clothes for the job you want, not the job you have!" The examples in this book will help you get the job you want and not be stuck in the job you have. Sylvie explains that attractive people earn 3–4 percent more than people with below-average looks. She adds that people also instantly and subconsciously look for trustworthiness. This is especially common and sought after in the health care world.

If you are in private practice, *you* represent your practice, so do it well. If you are working in an institution, *you* represent the institution, so do your homework and show up like you already work there. Predictability, along with consistency, is the cornerstone of what people see in seven seconds, which is not a lot of time to tell your story, so use visual cues to alert them of your true intentions.

I have a saying, "Data always wins!" We have a group of doctors in Activator Methods who have worked very hard to become Proficiency Rated in the AMCT. They are awarded the right to appear on our website. We send new patients to this group, over 17,000 of them each month. We also have a group that is referred to as a "Premium Page" and includes a picture of the chiropractor and their practice. This group receives twice as many hits on its web page simply because the patients want to see what the doctor looks like and what the staff looks like.

We have the data to prove this. This is all part of the "seven-second rule," where a patient decides who to put their trust in.

Leaders look confident; women are judged more by their weight and men by their height. Now age, contrary to popular opinion, has no direct correlation with success. I have been at both ends of this scale. As a young practitioner, I had "energy," and as a mature practitioner I have "confidence." As the book says, simply own your age.

I took my wife to a prominent orthopedic surgeon in Phoenix, Arizona, the hip replacement capital of the West. We never saw him dressed in anything but scrubs! He was very professional and looked like an orthopedist. It really gets down to trust.

I read an article that showed the highest trusted health care providers were nurses at 78 percent, dentists at 59 percent, general practitioners at 56 percent, and chiropractors at 33 percent. I am a chiropractor, and for years I have lectured students telling them a lot of the concepts in this book. Unfortunately, my profession lags behind when it comes to image, therefore trust!

Another thing you should know is your audience. I will tell a story of this importance. If you recall, I am from a small farming community in Minnesota. You have to speak their language, or you will lose their trust. I had a young chiropractic associate who was from the big city of New Jersey. He asked a patient who had come into the clinic, a farmer, how he had hurt himself. The farmer replied, "I fell off my silo." The young doctor said, "What is a silo?" When I saw the patient, he told me that he did not want to see the young doctor. I politely asked him, "Why?" He said, "If he doesn't know what a silo is, how can he know anything about my back problem?" It all came down to trust and knowing your audience.

Another topic that I found profound in Sylvie's book is that of leaders in a digital landscape. Today, we have to be careful about what we say on social media platforms. I am very careful to not use profanity. I warn students about the content of their Facebook pages. Furthermore, I am cautious about what is in the background of my home office during live streaming. All of these things I learned from Sylvie's seminars.

The Image of Leadership in Health Care   13

Activator Methods has been in business for 58 years, and people ask me how we stayed in business for that long. My answer is, we play by the book. And as *The Image of Leadership in Health Care* reiterates, if you have problems, consult with the correct expert. We have used a law firm for 30 years, and by following the attorneys' advice, we have avoided many lawsuits. This section of the book is very invaluable.

In conclusion, if you want to avoid pitfalls in leadership or professionalism and maintain a good reputation with as few mistakes as possible, then I highly recommend you read this book! Take notes, and good luck!

Dr. Arlan W. Fuhr
Chairman/Founder Activator Methods International Ltd.

Introduction

Welcome to *The Image of Leadership in Health Care*. The title reflects the reality that everyone can and should acknowledge, which is that true leadership manifests itself in ways that are both seen and unseen. They're equally important. While all leaders have their own individual styles and personalities, it cannot be doubted that the most effective leaders who succeed over a long period of time are seen and accepted because their interior skills and exterior images are in perfect alignment. In other words, what you see is what you get. As leaders, they're consistent and dependable, and their professional imprint—which I'll introduce to you later in the book—is strong and durable.

Whether you're already in a leadership role within the health care system, just embarking on your professional journey, or seeking to foster leadership among your staff, you might wonder, is this book for me?

My answer is that this book is definitely for you. It's crafted not only for the seasoned health care executive or the aspiring leader but also for those who make up the essential backbone of any health care institution: your team members. It's designed to instill a culture of professionalism and leadership at every level.

The principles laid out here hold true across all levels of health care management and leadership. Advancement is a constant pursuit, whether you're a seasoned department head aiming for an executive director position within a hospital, a senior nurse considering a leap into health care administration, or a specialist doctor with sights set on a chairperson role on a medical board. You must embody the qualities of these roles well in advance. Being seen as "leadership potential," someone who can handle the next tier of responsibilities and challenges, is crucial. Just as a senator might aspire to the presidency, health care professionals must also project the competence and confidence expected of the positions they aim to hold. The dynamics might vary—navigating the intricacies of medical hierarchy, the unwritten rules of hospital corridors, or the opening of your first practice—but the underlying truth remains: whether you're taking the first steps in your health care career or you're already leading from the front lines, the way you present yourself should be consistent with the leader you aim to be.

The drama in the emergency room, the critical conversations in private practice, the intensity in the operating theater, or the strategic decisions made in the executive suite—all these scenarios require leaders who have not only the expertise but also the professional gravitas to inspire confidence and drive change.

This book will take you step by step through the development of your professional imprint. The focus will be on all those things that people perceive about you, with an emphasis on your appearance and your image. I mean your image as you conduct a patient consultation, lead a health care team meeting, present at a medical conference, or engage in a panel interview for a new role. It's based on the proven concept that you cannot simply tell patients and colleagues that you're a leader and expect them to treat you as one.

You have to *show* people your leadership, every day, consistently, and in a way that encourages them to instantly accept you as someone in whom they will place their trust—and possibly their life.

We'll begin with the seven-second rule. This is that critical moment when others first encounter you, whether it's during a consultation with a patient's caregiver, as you step onto a ward, or during a clinical job interview. They may have some prior knowledge of you, but this is the first time they actually lay eyes on you. I'll show you how these people make up their minds very quickly about your leadership potential and either open the door for you or slam it shut. The good thing is that this process is entirely under your control. You can choose to present yourself as a leader or not.

Hence, I'll reveal the components of your professional imprint and how, after it's been established in those first seven seconds, you need to sustain it over time. I'll show you the ABCDEs of your professional imprint: appearance, behavior, communication, digital footprint, and environment.

While how you dress is very important, this is not a how-to book. I'm not going to detail specific items of clothing or accessories that you need to buy or wear. What I want to provide for you is a deep understanding of the concepts that you need to put into practice in your own way. I want to give you the power to create your own professional imprint that is true to your personality, that works for you for the duration of your career, and that also stands as a testament to the medical institution you're a part of and, by extension, the health care industry as a whole. Your attire is not just a personal statement but a symbol of the professionalism, dedication, and trust that embodies the spirit of health care.

Is this book going to stifle your personality? Absolutely not. The goal of this book is to remove unhelpful distractions that prevent people from seeing the leadership you can offer.

Leaders come in all shapes, sizes, ages, styles, or levels—including yours! This book can help you develop your professional imprint and become the leader you deserve to be. It's all a matter of letting people see the star that is ready to shine.

Let's get started on your exciting journey to achieving your full leadership potential.

Chapter 1
Seven Seconds

Seven Seconds:
Just a Glimpse, but the Vision Lasts.

1 2 3 **4 5 6 7**

Chapter 1: Seven Seconds

Appearance matters. Every hour of every day, we humans evaluate our environment based on what we see and hear. We avoid situations and people that seem threatening. We gravitate toward situations and people that appear welcoming. When we meet someone, we use sensory information to quickly determine if we're going to get along with them or if we need to keep our distance. We turn on the television and say, "This show looks good. I think I'll watch it." At the store, we inspect the food we want to buy. When a dog approaches on the street, before we extend our hand we look for its body language. Is the tail wagging, or is the dog tense?

Just as we judge others, we're judged by the people who meet us or see us in the media. Do we appear trustworthy? Confident? Or do we appear uncertain or detached? People whom we meet make quick decisions about us. Should they hire us? Vote for us? Buy something from us? Or in your case, should they entrust you with their care? Refer others to you? Follow your health recommendations?

Anyone who aspires to a position of leadership in any capacity needs to understand the power of image. The good news is that your image is something you can control. You can make it what you want. It's a combination of your dress, attitude, how you communicate online and offline, and the environment you operate in. These are all things you can shape and mold to work in your favor and help you rise to the level of leadership to which you aspire.

Let's start with a story. It's about two professionals who are applying for a key leadership role in a health care setting. They're competing for the position of chief medical officer at a prestigious hospital—a role that represents a significant step in their careers.

Their names are Charlie and Roger. For the sake of comparison, they're both men, but of course, they could just as easily both be women. While the story centers around getting hired, the principles revealed in the story are true across any situation: a doctor seeking to expand their clinic's services, a nurse aspiring to be promoted to a supervisory role, or a therapist presenting at a seminar.

First, let's meet Charlie. Brimming with the anticipation of securing the role, he waits in the reception area of the hospital's administrative wing. Dr. Judy, the hospital's CEO and president, comes into the reception area and greets him. With a warm yet professional smile, she extends her hand for a firm handshake, acknowledging his presence before guiding him to her office.

As they navigate the bustling hallway, passing by busy medical staff and patients, there's a thoughtful silence. Upon reaching her office, a quiet sanctuary compared to the lively corridors, Dr. Judy gestures for Charlie to take a seat. She then moves to her side of the desk, and with a brief smile, she scans his resumé. Her questions are straightforward. She inquires about his clinical experience and seeks to understand what unique contributions he envisions bringing to the hospital team.

During the interview, Charlie has an uneasy feeling. He doesn't think he's connecting with Dr. Judy. His credentials are solid—his resumé is what secured him this invitation—but he senses Dr. Judy is seeking something more—or something else. He feels the opportunity slipping away, like water through his fingers. He can't pinpoint the issue. Maybe, he speculates, Dr. Judy is simply methodical and reserved by nature. After all, she evaluates medical professionals regularly, and perhaps she's accustomed to maintaining a clinical distance, treating each candidate with the same measured scrutiny.

After twenty minutes, Dr. Judy closes Charlie's file and looks up. "Well, then, do you have any questions for me?" Charlie has a million questions, but the manager's coolness has him flustered. He replies that he doesn't have any questions before asking what the next step will be.

"As I'm sure you will understand," Dr. Judy says, "we've quite a few applicants for this position. This first round of interviews is just the beginning of the process. We'll be in touch next week. I want to thank you for your time and for your interest." She stands up and guides Charlie to the door. As Charlie walks out of the sliding doors of the hospital's administrative wing, he senses he's been hastily ushered out. His prospects for a callback, he thinks, are not very good.

Now let's see how Roger does during the same process. On paper, he has the same qualifications as Charlie. In fact, his resumé is identical to Charlie's.

As she did with Charlie, Dr. Judy greets Roger in the lobby of the hospital's main building. Her smile is warm and she extends a firm handshake, welcoming him before they start walking toward her office. Along the short walk through the bustling corridor, with staff moving briskly and the distant sounds of the intercom system, Dr. Judy engages him with questions. "Did you find your way here all right?" she inquires, followed by an offer: "Can I get you a water or coffee before we begin?"

Upon arriving at her office, she ushers Roger to a seat and then settles herself behind her desk. She regards Roger with a genuine smile and gives his resumé a cursory glance. His qualifications are clear. She delves into his professional history, inquiring what unique insights he could contribute to their institution.

When Roger brings up a current health care initiative the hospital is spearheading, Dr. Judy leans in, interested, and probes his approach to the project. Sensing an opportunity to deepen the conversation, she inquires if he'd be willing to discuss this further with the clinical director. Agreeable and eager, Roger affirms. A quick call is made, and shortly after, the clinical director arrives, allowing Roger to demonstrate his familiarity and expertise firsthand.

An hour after Roger first arrived, Dr. Judy says she really must excuse herself for another appointment, but is Roger free next week? Roger replies that he's available and thanks her for her time.

As Roger walks out of the sliding doors of the hospital's administrative wing, he feels like he's hit a home run. He made a solid connection with both the CEO and the president, Dr. Judy, and the clinical director. And he feels good about the next interview he's got lined up for today. It's a meeting across town with another leading health care institution, a direct competitor of the hospital.

At the medical staff meeting the next day, the panel reviews the candidates for the leadership role. Charlie's qualifications are considered first. "No," says Dr. Judy flatly. "He's not our type. He didn't seem confident. I can't see him joining our team." Then Roger's name is offered. "Very strong," says Judy. "I immediately got from him a sense of leadership. He has a dynamic personality. I think that if we hired him, he'd hit the ground running."

Charlie and Roger. Two qualified professionals with identical credentials. Yet in the eyes of Dr. Judy and the hiring committee, one emerged as less fitting, the other as a standout.

If you inquired with Dr. Judy about the distinguishing factor, she may not explicitly state that it was, for example, their attire that differentiated them. But in the health care environment, where professional presentation can be a reflection of attention to detail and conscientiousness, this indeed played a pivotal role in this example.

She may not admit her assessment of Charlie was formed within the initial moments of meeting him in the hospital's reception area, casually sitting in one of the waiting chairs, his posture relaxed to a fault, his eyes fixed unthinkingly on the screen of his mobile phone, barely acknowledging the busy hum around him. His attire, while not blatantly unprofessional, struck a note of casualness that seemed out of step with the hospital's professional atmosphere. His lack of alertness and engagement in the environment might have subtly conveyed a lack of preparedness or urgency that didn't align with the hospital's dynamic pace.

The interview? It might have been just an obligation. A formality. Charlie possibly never had a chance. As soon as she could, Dr. Judy cut the interview short and showed him the door. Despite Charlie's potential, he wasn't given a real chance.

The Image of Leadership in Health Care

In both recruitment and executive circles, the visual appearance and perception of a candidate or colleague is often an unspoken consideration. While it may be regarded as trivial and not acknowledged as part of the formal evaluation process, it nonetheless plays a part in decision making. Furthermore, legal and ethical standards prevent hiring committees from citing appearance as a reason for employment decisions. They won't explicitly say, "We can't bring you into our medical team because your presentation doesn't align with our expectations." Such a statement would cross professional boundaries and could lead to significant repercussions.

Health care recruiters may also not acknowledge that they possibly already have formed an opinion about a candidate before they even meet, influenced by the credentials and image presented in the application and by the candidate's online persona. Nonetheless, the reality is that in any environment or profession where professionalism is paramount, the impression made by one's appearance can subtly influence the final decision. And of course, the same principles hold true when it comes to patient care.

Your appearance matters every single time you interact with patients or their caregivers. In the health care setting, the way you present yourself can significantly affect the comfort and confidence levels of those you're treating or advising. A well considered, professional appearance conveys a sense of competence and reliability, fostering trust from the moment you enter the room. It's not merely about aesthetic appeal but about demonstrating respect for the profession and the people you serve.

Whether it's ensuring your scrubs are clean and well fitted, your badge is visible, or your demeanor reflects the seriousness and compassion of your role, each detail contributes to the overall environment. Every aspect of your presentation speaks volumes and can be as crucial to patient recovery and comfort as the medical advice or treatment you provide.

Everyone knows the old saying "You can't judge a book by its cover."

Yet the hard reality is that every day, in countless patient interactions, health care professionals are judged by their "covers"—whether it's scrubs or white coats in a hospital, business casual in a private practice, name badges, grooming, or even the practicality or quality of footwear.

It may not be fair, but it's an intrinsic human instinct. While we encourage looking beyond the surface, there often isn't enough time for others to form opinions based on deep observation. That's why the brain defaults to the path of least resistance, the most straightforward route for gathering information—through our eyes. Humans are, after all, visual creatures.

Research led by *Doug Vogel* at the University of Arizona illuminated the speed at which our brains process images, which is 60,000 times faster than text, and asserted that 90 percent of information is transmitted visually.

Further emphasizing the predominance of visual information, *Dr. Mary Potter* from MIT led a study that found the human brain can process images seen for as little as thirteen milliseconds. This rapid processing suggests our brains are constantly and efficiently working to understand the visual world around us. These astounding facts highlight the immediate impact of visual cues on our perception, making your appearance a powerful communication tool.

For health care leaders, this means their visual presentation can speak volumes before a word is uttered, impacting patient care, leadership perception, and the overall efficacy of health care delivery. A leader's appearance is not just a superficial layer but a crucial component of their professional imprint and how they're perceived within the micro-moments of first encounters.

Charlie might have believed his less-than-pristine attire and demeanor were acceptable based on his previous roles. However, the moment Dr. Judy saw him, her internal judgment was decisive. She possibly thought, "This candidate doesn't understand what our health care institution stands for. And I don't have time to teach him."

Of course, it's absolutely possible that in a more casual health care setting or a different medical department, Charlie's less formal attire could have been acceptable. However, for Dr. Judy's standards and the particular health care role he sought, it was not a fit.

The goal is to reflect an understanding of the environment you wish to join and show you can seamlessly integrate into the professional culture of the health care institution.

As for Roger, the moment Dr. Judy saw him—even before they shook hands—she knew he was a contender. His suit, his haircut, his choice of necktie, his flawless shoes—all spoke of a man who saw himself as a leader. But it was not vanity that was the source of Roger's impulse to look like a leader. He was no super-slick wannabe anchorman. In fact, his professional appearance was driven by confidence. His poised attentiveness set the stage. He stood prepared in the waiting area, embodying readiness and eagerness for the interview.

When Dr. Judy approached, his smile was broad, genuine—a silent yet eloquent greeting. He stepped forward, extending his hand first, initiating a handshake that was firm and assured. Each micro-expression and gesture, from his direct gaze to the confident tilt of his head, signaled a leader. These subtle cues, often overlooked, were the fibers weaving the macro impact on Dr. Judy's perception. His external presentation was a mirror of his internal readiness, and this congruence was not lost on her. It was the detail that turned a candidate into a contender.

Of course, Roger wanted to appear successful, but on a deeper level, he wanted to be instantly accepted into the hospital's culture. He wanted Dr. Judy to be able to look beyond his clothing and see he could contribute. He wanted to make his appearance a non-issue. He wanted her to instantly trust him and believe he could get the job done. He wanted to look like a leader. Not a pompous windbag, but someone who inspired confidence and who could bring out the very best in others.

The Cost of a Poor Professional Imprint

While it's your duty to maintain a positive professional identity, it's understood that perfection is unattainable, and everyone, even in health care leadership, is prone to missteps. Some errors may pass without much notice, but others could become widely known, perhaps through a viral social media post. It could be a lapse in decorum at a hospital fundraiser, an inadvertently shared joke that doesn't sit well publicly, or a day when your attire might not meet the expected standards of your health care role. Not upholding the highest professional standards in every aspect of your work can result in significant consequences such as the following:

- **Lower patient satisfaction:** A professional's appearance can affect patient perceptions, potentially leading to decreased satisfaction and trust.

- **Loss of respect from peers:** Colleagues may find it hard to respect health care professionals who do not present themselves appropriately, impacting teamwork.

- **Distraction from patient care:** An inappropriate appearance can become a distraction, diverting attention from the primary focus of providing quality health care.

- **Harmful stereotypes:** Unprofessional attire or behavior can reinforce negative stereotypes, which may harm a health care professional's career trajectory.

- **Missed promotions:** Failing to present a professional identity may result in being overlooked for promotions or special assignments, limiting career growth.

- **Financial consequences:** A lack of professionalism could mean losing patients, directly impacting revenue.

- **Undermining of professional boundaries:** Inappropriate attire can blur the lines of professional boundaries, increasing the risk of complaints or accusations.

- **Workplace hostility:** A lack of professionalism can contribute to an environment where disrespect or bullying may thrive, affecting morale and workplace culture.

You think this sounds far-fetched? Think again. Especially in today's digital landscape, the reach and influence of social media on professional reputations are profound, with health care professionals being particularly vulnerable. Actions and comments that once might have remained private can now lead to public outcry and professional downfall.

An ER doctor at a New York hospital faced intense backlash after sharing insensitive political content, praising Hamas's music festival massacre on her social media. The incident not only sparked a public furor but also brought into question the physician's professional judgment.

Another ER doctor at a Rhode Island hospital found her career compromised over a Facebook post that, while not naming the patient, provided enough detail to breach confidentiality. This indiscretion led to her termination and a fine, highlighting the critical importance of privacy in patient care.

At a hospital in Los Gatos, a contract doctor's dismissive treatment of a patient's condition was captured and disseminated online, leading to her suspension. The viral video tarnished the reputation of both the individual and the institution.

In New York City, a hospital worker's argument with her children over a personal matter outside her workplace escalated when recorded and shared online, culminating in her suspension and a whirlwind of negative social media attention.

These examples serve as cautionary tales, illustrating the heightened stakes for health care professionals in an era where social media can amplify personal misjudgments into career-altering events.

It often takes just one moment (or one simple click) and your image is instantly destroyed. And while the examples I've provided may illustrate severe repercussions, it's important to remember that we're all prone to human error. Your own lapses, while not as consequential, are part of the shared human experience. Mistakes will happen; it's an unavoidable aspect of life.

Nobody is perfect, after all. We all have off-days. We all are humans. We aren't robots. You're not always going to have those first seconds picture-perfectly laid out. You're not always going to choose the right outfit, right attitude, right words. You're not always going to be confident, prepared, or able to do what's expected of you. However, what you *can* do is to always try your best and realize that an initial impression is just that—a beginning.

Chapter 2
Your Professional Imprint

The Indelible Mark
Etched in Others' Minds.

Chapter 2:
Your Professional Imprint

Let's begin with some clarity on the lingo. Terms abound in this context. Some might refer to it as "executive presence" or "professional image," others might use "professional identity," and there are those who speak of "personal branding." Each term, while distinct, converges on a core principle: the essence of how you present and define yourself in your career.

Yet it's the initial interaction, this "professional imprint," that etches your reputation into the minds of others. It's a moment as brief as it's lasting, that enduring mark you make in the minds of others during those initial fleeting moments, where the ephemeral dance of first impressions sets the stage for the enduring narrative of your professional saga. This professional imprint is more than just a first impression; it's the genesis of your reputation, the spark that ignites the perception of your image, identity, and brand in the workplace.

It's quick and indelible. Some studies suggest it takes seven, three, or eleven seconds, and they delineate different characteristics you're judged on. In my professional work, I've focused on the study that implies it takes place within seven seconds. However, to be honest, the exact length of time doesn't really matter as much.

What matters more is that this happens automatically in our brains—no matter whether we're aware of it, no matter whether we find it fair or not, and no matter whether, under our shabby clothes, we've the soul of Mother Theresa.

Our professional imprint is a direct reflection of the attention and care we invest in our most valuable asset: ourselves. It's evident in the meticulous choices we make, from the polished shoes that carry us through the day to the precision with which we assemble our attire, mindful of its symbolism and functionality in our respective roles. It's in the deliberate selection of accessories that convey professionalism without compromising on personal expression. Do we allow ourselves the luxury of time to ensure our appearance is immaculate, from the neatness of our nails to the subtleties of our scent? Do we pause to consider the state of our tools and instruments, ensuring they're as pristine as our personal presentation?

These are the significant, yet often unspoken, elements that contribute to our professional imprint. Each detail is a thread in the fabric of the impression we weave, not only benefitting our self-image but also enhancing the esteem of the institutions we represent.

The reputation of any health care institution—whether it's a hospital, private clinic, outpatient center, research laboratory, or your own practice—is significantly influenced by the appearance and conduct of its staff, including you. Every health care professional, from the receptionist at a family clinic to the lead surgeon at a top hospital, must offer patients, caregivers, or colleagues the best possible representation of themselves.

A health care entity understands that its staff members, whether they're part of a large hospital network or a single-doctor practice, embody the institution's values and ethos. It's crucial that their initial interactions with the medical and nonmedical community foster the most positive image of their dedication and professionalism. As such, maintaining a professional appearance is essential in demonstrating their commitment to quality care and patient satisfaction.

While our story of Charlie and Roger centered around a job interview, the so-called seven-second rule applies in countless everyday situations, including health care interactions. Whether you're greeting a new patient, consulting with colleagues, participating in a telemedicine call, presenting a case study, or attending a health care networking event, your professional imprint is established almost instantly. Once an opinion is formed, altering it can be an uphill battle.

When Dr. Judy first encountered Charlie and mentally relegated him to the "unsuitable" category, the possibility of reversing that impression was slim. Right from the outset, his opportunity had slipped away.

The encounter between Dr. Judy and Charlie could have unfolded under numerous health care scenarios. They could have been meeting in a consultation room, with Charlie as a new health care consultant pitching a quality improvement plan. Or perhaps Charlie could have been a medical sales representative seeking Dr. Judy's endorsement for a new piece of medical equipment. The context is irrelevant; within a few seconds, based on his presentation, Charlie would have been relegated to the "doubtful" category.

Conversely, when Dr. Judy encountered Roger, his professional imprint immediately positioned him as a credible and competent individual. From that instant, he was in the running to achieve whatever goal he had set out for. He had become a viable candidate, and the likelihood was on his side. This is the aspiration of any professional: to be immediately perceived as competent and capable, thereby optimizing every opportunity to showcase your leadership and expertise in the field.

Your attire shapes not only how you're perceived by others but also how you perceive yourself. Looking the part can significantly enhance your ability to act the part. For health care professionals, this means dressing in a manner that communicates confidence, competence, and compassion, whether you're in the hospital or clinic or conducting virtual consultations.

Dressing affects your mindset and, as a result, your productivity and quality of interactions. It involves mirroring the respect for your role and the care you provide, even if it's through a screen. This is not just about the clothes; it includes embodying the professional leader you are.

It's not about donning power suits or clinical attire unnecessarily but about finding that middle ground where you feel and project your professional best.

Society's preoccupation with, and marketing of, physical attractiveness reinforces the assumption that being good-looking pays bigger benefits. And the undeniable truth is that being attractive can be a huge asset.

Many of these studies are summarized and discussed in the 2011 book *Beauty Pays: Why Attractive People Are More Successful*, written by *Daniel Hamermesh*, an economist at the University of Texas in Austin. Hamermesh reviews research that shows attractive people earn an average of 3 or 4 percent more than people with below-average looks. These professionals are also hired sooner, get promotions more quickly, are higher-ranking in their companies, and get all kinds of extra benefits. Why? It turns out more attractive people often bring more money to their companies and are therefore more valuable employees.

In the health care environment, the influence of physical appearance and the societal focus on attractiveness, as Hamermesh discusses in his book, is also evident. Although health care is a sector primarily concerned with the well-being and treatment of patients, the principles highlighted by Hamermesh's research do not exclude this field.

I'm not talking about your DNA. It's not about how tall you are or your body type, although this plays a role, as you will find out later in this book. I'm talking about the countless things you can do—regardless of the qualities bestowed upon you by the vagaries of the genetic lottery—to develop your best qualities (we all have them!) and minimize your liabilities (we all have them too!).

Imprinting can be demonstrated easily. When I speak at an event, I usually enter the stage and count out loud to seven, demonstrating how fleeting yet critical this moment in time is for setting the tone of the audience's perception. Then I open up the plethora of decisions they possibly already made about me without knowing anything about my background, skills, knowledge, or the value I bring to the event at this point.

The research I rely on in my work is based on a study conducted by psychologist *Michael Solomon*, back when he was at NYU.

It suggests our initial imprint is not based on a single element; instead, it is a composite of at least eleven different elements that people subconsciously judge within those first seven seconds of meeting us. These elements include your:

1. Socioeconomic level
2. Education level
3. Competence and honesty, believability, and perceived credibility
4. Sex role identification
5. Level of sophistication
6. Trustworthiness
7. Level of success
8. Ethnicity
9. Religious background
10. Political background
11. Social/sexual/professional desirability

Yet it's imperative to approach this list with a discerning mind. On one enlightening occasion, I had the honor of engaging with Dr. Solomon in a conversation, and he shared a significant point: like many scientific findings, the interpretations of his study have been bent to fit various narratives across the Internet and by self-proclaimed experts. It's one of those pervasive myths that human judgment rigidly conforms to this eleven-elements-and-seven-seconds rule.

However, for Dr. Judy, for example, assessing prospective health care team members, the same principle applies as in any industry: certain elements such as sex role identification, ethnicity, religious and political background, or sexual desirability should not influence her judgment and are ethically required to hold no sway in professional evaluations. However, attributes such as competence, honesty, believability, credibility, and trustworthiness become paramount. Dr. Judy's initial assessment of Charlie's and Roger's presentations led her to subconsciously categorize them based on critical professional qualities.

In contrast, if you're introduced to a potential romantic partner, the imprint values will be rearranged. In such a situation, their social/sexual/professional desirability will probably leap to the top of the list, along with sex role identification.

Should these aspects not align with our expectations, our view of all other attributes might be subtly tinted. While one might hope these initial impressions could evolve and change over time, most of us know how challenging it can be to reshape this first opinion. These impressions are the lens through which all subsequent qualities are filtered, and not acknowledging these early signals can lead to difficulties in any potential relationship. We might find ourselves grappling with the consequences of overlooking those initial, instinctive cues.

The Science of First Impressions

In an industry as deeply rooted in evidence-based practice as health care, professionals are adept at navigating and interpreting a myriad of scientific studies. So with this perspective of rigorous scrutiny and application, let me introduce you to just one more of the many studies on first impressions—keeping in mind that while this is a singular example, it reflects a broader consensus within the scientific community about the impact and lasting power of those critical first seconds.

In 2009, neuroscientists at New York University and Harvard University identified the neural systems involved in forming first impressions of others. Their study, which shows how we encode social information and then evaluate it in making initial judgments, was conducted in the laboratory of *Elizabeth Phelps* and reported in the journal *Nature Neuroscience*.

The study was based on the concept that each new person whom we meet presents a set of ambiguous and complex information. Because it's a first meeting, the information is primarily visual, although other senses—hearing, smell, and even touch if you shake hands—can come into play.

We quickly sort through this information and judge whether we're attracted to that person or not. It's an ancient and deeply embedded process that allowed our ancestors to quickly assess their relationship to a new person: Friend or foe? Social superior or inferior? And perhaps most significantly, will this person be useful to the group—a leader—or will they be a burden and consume more than they contribute?

But how does this complex process happen? The study sought to investigate the brain mechanisms that give rise to impressions formed immediately after meeting a new person.

To explore the process of first impression formation, the researchers designed an experiment in which they examined the brain activity when participants made initial evaluations of fictional individuals. The researchers gave participants written profiles of twenty individuals with different personality traits. The profiles, presented along with pictures of these fictional individuals, included scenarios indicating both positive (e.g., intelligent) and negative (e.g., lazy) traits in their depictions.

After reading the profiles, the participants were asked to evaluate how much they liked or disliked each profiled individual. These impressions varied depending on how much each participant valued the different positive and negative traits conveyed. For instance, if a participant liked intelligence in a partner more than they disliked laziness, they might form a positive impression of someone.

During this impression formation period, the researchers observed the brain activity of the participants using functional magnetic resonance imaging (fMRI). Based on the participants' responses, the researchers were able to measure the difference in brain activity when they encountered information that was more important in forming the first impression.

During the encoding of impression-relevant information, the neuroimaging results revealed significant activity in two regions of the brain. The first, the posterior cingulate cortex (PCC), has been linked to making economic decisions and assigning subjective value to rewards.

The second, the amygdala, is a small structure in the medial temporal lobe that previously has been linked to emotional learning about inanimate objects, as well as social evaluations based on trust or race group. In the study, these parts of the brain showed increased activity when encoding information that was consistent with the impression.

The study suggested that when we only briefly encounter others and have limited and ambiguous cues to evaluate, brain regions that are important in emotional learning and value representation are engaged. When encoding everyday social information during a social encounter, these regions sort information based on its personal and subjective significance and summarize it into a single value—that is, a first initial imprint. Thus, we can say that our emotional learning + our values = the person's imprint.

And this imprint is multidimensional, extending its influence far beyond the initial point of contact. It's an intricate interplay of personal and professional signals that collectively shape the narrative of our professional existence.

It's not a static or isolated occurrence; it's a dynamic force that echoes across various facets of our professional landscape. It's the subtle yet powerful undercurrent that can sway decisions, alter interactions, and steer the course of our professional journeys.

As we unpack the significance of this imprint, let's explore how it reverberates.

Consider the impact on yourself. When you project confidence and competence, you're more likely to feel empowered and capable in your role. This self-assurance can translate into improved performance.

Reflect on your familial and social circle. The way you present yourself professionally not only influences yourself but also extends to the perceptions of your family and social networks. It can establish a halo of trust and respect that permeates your entire support network.

Think about those you interact with. Patients, colleagues, and stakeholders form their initial impressions of you based on various factors, including your appearance. By presenting yourself in a positive manner, you inspire trust and credibility, fostering stronger relationships and better outcomes.

Acknowledge the institution you represent. Whether you're working in a hospital, running your own practice, or collaborating with other health care professionals, your appearance reflects not only on yourself but also on the reputation of your institution. By upholding high standards of professionalism and integrity, you contribute to the positive image and reputation of your medical institution.

Evaluate the industry-wide implications. Your individual professional imprint also casts a wider net, affecting the collective image of the health care industry. This, in turn, can lead to increased trust in health care services, bolstering the community's willingness to engage with and support medical institutions and initiatives.

Therefore, it's essential to be mindful of how you present yourself in every interaction because it can have far-reaching effects.

The Sustained Imprint

Your first imprint is only the beginning. It needs to evolve into a lasting positive impression. I call this the "sustained imprint."

I once developed and organized a leadership seminar for a group of twenty high potentials from the retail and tourism company I worked for. The participants were quite surprised to find out their trainer was not a person; instead, we trained them with the help of horses.

In one of the first exercises, we split the participants into two groups. The first group went into the riding area, where an unleashed horse was waiting for them.

The participants were told to walk in straight with confident steps, to appear strong, to keep eye contact with the horse, and to keep a straight face. When they arrived at the horse, they had to smack their horsewhips on the ground several times. The horse immediately began to run in a circle. The participants whipped and whipped, and they were briefed to stop when the horse appeared to be tired.

When they put aside the whip, something rather "magical" happened: the horse followed them everywhere. Participants walked around the horse arena, and their assigned horse happily trotted after them. None of the participants had said one word to the horse. The horse just followed.

The second group received a different briefing. They were supposed to walk in and appear friendly and kind to the horse. They were told to motivate the horse by petting it, talking to it, and developing a relationship. They even brought in treats and encouraged the horse with all their hearts.

The first observation we made was that they had a really hard time making the horse run in a circle. It was obvious the horse wanted more treats and more tender loving care. Not much happened. The horse didn't follow and at one point didn't even come back for more treats because, obviously, there were no more.

What did we learn? Horses, much like people, respond to the nonverbal cues of confidence and assertiveness. The first group's authoritative approach, conveyed through their posture, gaze, and decisive actions, left a compelling imprint on the horses, commanding respect and prompting a clear behavioral response.

This underscores the power of a strong initial presence; without uttering a single word, their commanding demeanor set the tone for the interaction, resulting in the horses' compliance and subsequent allegiance.

We also observed that the first group, emboldened by their initial success, celebrated with a sense of triumph, embodying the spirit of leadership and victory. However, as time progressed, the complexity of their challenge unfolded. They began to display inconsistency in their demeanor and actions.

To the horse, their once clear and commanding presence became unpredictable. And predictability, along with consistency, is the cornerstone of leadership—it's what engenders trust and respect. We seek reliability in leaders' words and decisions and in the steadiness of their conduct.

The first group, while initially successful in commanding the horse's attention, failed to uphold the robustness of that initial impression. They did not succeed in cultivating it into a sustained imprint. The horse's diminishing response was a clear testament to the group's faltering consistency. The lesson was vivid and unequivocal: a leader's impact is measured not only by the strength of their initial presence but also by the enduring imprint they manage to sustain over time.

The game isn't over after seven seconds. Outstanding leaders leave lasting impressions by how they look and how they present themselves, always and everywhere—consistently. Like Roger's experience, the positive imprint developed in mere seconds only gets you in the door. It makes the possibility of acceptance very real. It breaks down the barrier between you and the person you meet.

Conversely, the negative impression that Charlie created caused the door to slam shut. It reduced the possibility of acceptance and created a barrier between him and the person he met—who, in this case, had the power to either help him up the ladder of success or pass him by in favor of someone else.

The principles of sustained impressions hold true with even greater significance in health care environments. In the bustling corridors of a hospital, the steadfast composure and consistent professionalism of a physician or nurse can transform patient interactions from mere medical transactions to experiences of compassionate care.

From the emergency room to the recovery ward, the way health care professionals carry themselves—amidst the urgency and unpredictability—can foster an atmosphere of trust and safety.

In the more intimate setting of a private practice, the sustained imprint is equally critical. From the moment a patient steps into the waiting area, every detail contributes to the patient's experience. The welcoming smile of the receptionist, the thoughtful décor of the office, and the attentive presence of the practitioner all coalesce to create a healing environment. It's the consistent warmth in the greeting, the unwavering attentiveness during consultations, and the reliability of follow-up care that solidifies a practitioner's reputation.

Whether in a high-stakes environment where quick decisions are paramount or in a private clinic where personalized attention is key, the health care professional's ability to maintain a consistent, positive professional imprint is not just preferred—it's essential. It's what turns first-time patients into lifelong clients and what upholds the honor and trust inherent in the health care profession.

You might question whether the continuity of this positive, sustained imprint is solely contingent upon our appearance. Clearly, it's not the sole factor, yet it's significant. Your appearance, throughout the entire process, acts as a critical filter through which all your professional behaviors and communication are perceived. It's a silent but powerful language that precedes and punctuates our every action. It sets the stage upon which our competencies are judged. While not the entire story, it's an essential chapter in the narrative of our professional identity.

There's a famous study by *Albert Mehrabian* that suggests that the words you say—the *actual words*, not the tone or inflection—account for only 7 percent of the imprint you make. It's called the 7 percent—38 percent—55 percent rule. Words account for 7 percent, tone of voice accounts for 38 percent, and body language accounts for 55 percent of the imprint you make.

One might think (or might have heard) this study suggests it's not important what you say or how you behave; it's only about appearance. Of course, that's just not true. It's another Internet myth, and Mehrabian himself made countless attempts to clarify that the study cannot be interpreted this way.

Still, countless coaches, trainers, and speakers use this study to suggest the only thing that matters is appearance, neglecting the significance of verbal communication and behavior in creating a lasting impression.

However, if you have only seven seconds to make an excellent first impression, your appearance takes on greater importance. Many people do not even have the chance to use their behavior and communication for a powerful first impression.

You'll recall that Charlie and Roger had identical resumés. (This is not hypothetical; in today's competitive job marketplace, among dozens of qualified applicants for a given position, there are bound to be several candidates who look the same on paper.) The chances are good that when Dr. Judy first met them and they had a conversation—that is, during the first few seconds—there wasn't much difference in the actual words they spoke.

Those initial moments are simply too fleeting to demonstrate one's verbal prowess. Instead, in such brief encounters, it's our visual and perhaps even our sensed presence that speaks volumes. The human brain, in its quest for instant understanding, relies primarily on the visual cues it receives, complemented by the subtle undercurrents of what it feels rather than what it hears.

As Charlie and Roger awaited their turns in the waiting area, silent narratives unfolded within mere moments of Dr. Judy's approach. They cast a long and sometimes indelible shadow, setting a stage where unseen forces came into play. These forces, subtly yet powerfully, influenced the trajectory of Dr. Judy's judgments. Like invisible threads, they pulled at the fabric of perception, weaving assumptions and conclusions based on the initial visual encounter. These energies, silent but potent, elevated Roger in a halo of positive light and shrouded Charlie in a cloud of skepticism.

For you, navigating this landscape with awareness and finesse can turn the tide of unconscious judgments in your favor, cementing a reputation that stands resilient through time.

The Invisible Filters of Perception

Put yourself into the shoes of a patient, for just a moment. You find yourself needing quick medical care, and as you enter a practice, a sea of expectations and anxieties floods your mind. The receptionist is busy typing, not noticing you right away. As seconds tick by—which seem to feel like an eternity—you start to feel a bit ignored.

During that time, your eyes wander, and you can't help but notice the receptionist's nails look like they could use some attention. Their makeup and hair seem a bit much for such an early hour. When they finally do greet you, your patience has worn thin. You were on time, but now they've left you waiting. Finally, sitting down in the waiting room, you spot a crumpled piece of paper under a chair —missed by the cleaners, perhaps. The chairs around you show signs of age, with cracks and worn edges. Then, as you're called to see the doctor, a strange smell drifts from the staff room. Maybe they just had lunch?

The doctor comes to get you, moving quickly, not stopping for introductions or handshakes. Their shoes have seen better days, and their white coat has lost some of its brightness. All these little things add up in your mind, painting a picture of a place that might not be up to the mark. "No wonder," you think to yourself. "This seems to be the standard in this practice"—a standard that feels lacking.

What you just experienced is the powerful influence of unconscious biases leading your mind to make snap judgments. The sights and impressions, from the receptionist's appearance to the subtle cues of the environment, all funnel through your perceptions, coloring your expectations—possibly even without a word being spoken.

These biases are like silent storytellers, weaving narratives that may not necessarily be accurate or fair. However, they set the stage for your experience, and as we peel back the layers, you'll see how these hidden scripts can shape our interactions and decisions in profound ways.

Unconscious biases are mental shortcuts or patterns of thinking that influence perceptions without conscious awareness. These biases are often based on social stereotypes, personal experiences, or cultural norms.

Confirmation bias, for example, is one of the most prominent unconscious biases. Confirmation bias is a psychological phenomenon in which individuals favor information that confirms their preexisting beliefs or hypotheses. It's the tendency to seek out information in a way that validates our existing perceptions. This means we're more likely to notice details that support what we already think, often overlooking evidence to the contrary.

From the moment you walked through the door of this practice, your brain was picking up on cues and details that began to form an impression. When the receptionist didn't immediately look up, their unpolished appearance confirmed any lurking thoughts that the practice is disorganized or unprofessional. Each subsequent observation, from the crumpled paper to the worn furniture and the doctor's hurried entrance, built upon this initial judgment.

Instead of seeing these as isolated instances, confirmation bias leads you to interpret them as part of a pattern, reinforcing the belief that the practice does not meet the standards of care you expect. Each detail seems to "confirm" your initial impression, and this bias can be particularly challenging to overcome once it takes root.

Anchoring bias is another pervasive mental shortcut we often take in which we rely too heavily on the first piece of information we receive about a subject—the "anchor"—and allow it to disproportionately influence our subsequent judgments and decisions.

Once an anchor is set, other interpretations and information, even if more relevant or factual, tend to be viewed through the lens of this initial reference point.

Suppose the initial delay and the receptionist's disheveled appearance were the first bits of information you registered. These details likely became your anchor. As you continued to wait, even before noticing the crumpled paper or the smell from the staff room, your mind was already anchored to the notion that this practice was subpar. This early anchor had an impact on your entire perception of the care provided, regardless of the actual quality of the medical services you received.

The **horn effect** leads us to attribute negative characteristics based on a single perceived flaw, causing us to view all traits of an individual or entity negatively. For example, the receptionist's posture, which could be neutral or simply a product of a long day, might seem to you to indicate a lack of interest or enthusiasm. This bias can lead you to overlook any instances of competence or moments of kindness, focusing instead on these traits that seem to confirm your initial negative impression.

Negativity bias is another cognitive phenomenon in which negative aspects have a more significant impact on an individual's psychological state than do neutral or positive things. Essentially, we tend to pay more attention to, and give more weight to, negative experiences or information.

Did you even notice the receptionist's meticulous attire? The effort they put into carefully documenting patient cases, a sign of thoroughness and dedication? Did you observe the efficiency with which they eventually handled your paperwork or the accuracy in their data entry? Similarly, the doctor's speed may have been a reflection of their ability to manage a busy practice effectively, ensuring every patient receives timely care.

However, these positive traits may have been eclipsed by the more immediate negative judgments, steering your overall impression toward the unfavorable due to the negativity bias.

And even after you've left the practice, unconscious biases continue to steer your mind.

Availability bias ensures you overestimate the likelihood or importance of certain events or outcomes based on their ease of recall or availability in memory. This means the negative aspects you noticed loom larger in your memory than the positive ones. They become the ready examples that come to mind when you reflect on the visit or discuss it with others.

This tendency can extend to the point where you might find yourself at home browsing online reviews of the practice, unconsciously searching for further confirmation of your initial opinion. As you skim through numerous positive testimonials, they barely register; instead, your attention zeroes in on the few critical remarks. These resonate with your experience, reinforcing your perspective. Feeling validated, you consider it almost a duty to add your own critique to the mix.

Welcome to the **bandwagon effect** in action—a bias that compels us to adopt beliefs or behaviors because they seem popular or because others are doing it. In this context, the critical comments of others echo your own impressions, and the weight of collective criticism may feel like an undeniable proof, further solidifying your initial judgments.

The **Dunning-Kruger effect** may also take hold as you consider leaving a review. Feeling qualified to evaluate the entire medical staff after a single visit, this bias overstates your own expertise, leading you to assert judgments that might not reflect the true caliber of the healthcare professionals' skills and services.

Sunk cost fallacy may cause you to persist in viewing the practice negatively because you've already invested in visits and treatments there, despite there being evidence of good care in the future.

I could go on and on. At the moment of writing this book, science is aware of approximately 185 biases that influence the human mind.

These biases work beneath the surface of consciousness and affect every aspect of our lives, from the mundane to the critical, without us even realizing it. Understanding these biases is key to navigating the complex landscape of human thought and perception, allowing us to make more informed and deliberate choices.

And while unconscious biases can have a harmful and pervasive effect—manifesting in serious issues like workplace harassment and obstructing diversity efforts—they also play a role in the brief window in which perceptions are formed and professional imprints are made. In this narrow but critical space, you can harness the power of these biases to your advantage.

By being aware of them and intentionally presenting yourself in a manner that aligns positively from the very first moment with these cognitive shortcuts, you can influence others to see you in a more favorable light along the way. This doesn't mean manipulating perceptions dishonestly but rather ensuring the genuine and best aspects of your professional identity are what shine through and resonate the most.

For the practice we just visited, if, upon your arrival, the receptionist had briefly looked up and acknowledged you with a smile, making it clear they were wrapping up important work for another patient's care, your impression might have been different.

Maybe they could have offered you a glass of water or a cup of coffee while you had to wait. Their unkempt nails maybe would have faded into the background, overshadowed by their meticulous attire and the courtesy of their instant greeting. You might have thought to yourself, "They're really dedicated to each patient's privacy and care."

As you took your seat, the receptionist's professionalism might have cast a positive light on the surroundings, making the waiting room's imperfections seem less significant; instead, you might have noticed the beautiful paintings by a local artist on the wall. When the doctor arrived promptly, their efficient manner could have been seen as a sign of a well-run practice that values your time, turning a potentially negative first impression into a positive reflection of the practice's standards.

However, using unconscious biases to your advantage is not accomplished by making just a good impression; it requires crafting an exceptional one. To stand out in a sea of sameness is to go above and beyond the expected, to offer the unexpected in ways that positively disrupt and dismantle preconceived notions. It's about embodying excellence in every action, every interaction, turning the ordinary into the memorable.

The question, then, isn't simply about being noticed—it demands being unforgettable. How can you truly stand out? The answer lies not just in what we do but in how we do it—with intention, with difference, with a touch of the remarkable in the everyday.

Stand Out for the Right Reasons

In the competitive landscape of health care, where the stakes are as high as the well-being of human lives, the concept of standing out becomes not just a personal ambition but a professional imperative. The truth is, in a field driven by innovation and trust, good doesn't cut it anymore; "good" is the baseline, the expectation. To be a leader in health care—to truly make an impact—you can't afford to simply fit the mold. Average blends in, and by blending in, you become invisible.

Think of the game of Tetris for a moment. For some readers, Tetris is a nostalgic nod to the past, a digital relic from the days of clunky, handheld gaming devices. For others, perhaps of a younger generation, it's a classic that's been rediscovered on smartphones and modern gaming platforms. No matter the version you're familiar with, the metaphor stands: each piece that falls is designed to fit perfectly into a space, completing a line. The goal is to rotate and align falling blocks to complete lines.

But what happens when the line is completed? It disappears. This is a triumph in Tetris, but in your career, it's a warning. When you align too perfectly with the patterns already in play, you risk becoming part of the background—another completed line that serves its purpose and then vanishes in the sea of sameness.

In health care, when leaders stand out, they do so by transcending the ordinary. They become the piece in Tetris that not only fits but also starts a reaction, changing the landscape, challenging the status quo, and bringing new possibilities into play. Standing out means being the architect of change, the beacon of innovation, and the embodiment of exceptional care. This requires being the memorable piece that doesn't just fill a gap but also creates a new path for others to follow.

You might be thinking, "Well, is it really always good to stand out?" For a pop star, standing out from the crowd in any way they can will always bring positive returns. Whatever gets their name mentioned in the press will help sell their records. For an entertainer, standing out from the crowd, regardless of the reason, is good to an extent. If they get on the evening news simply because everybody thinks they have done something out of order, they've won the game.

But in the professional universe, standing out for its own sake is a terrible idea. In the professional space, there's a *great* way to stand out and there's a *bad* way to stand out.

The surest path to standing out in the best way is to consistently do three things:

- First, be your very best self, bringing your unique strengths and personality to the forefront.
- Second, embody and uphold the highest values of your institution, serving as a living testament to its mission and principles.
- And third, don't just meet expectations—surpass them. Strive to go above and beyond what's anticipated, delivering extraordinary care and consideration that's not just good but exceptional.

The bad way to stand out is . . . well, any other way.

It's this commitment to excellence that will distinguish you in a profession where excellence is the most valued currency.

Imagine when you walk into a practice, you're greeted not just by a friendly receptionist but also by a wave of innovation. The receptionist, with a welcoming nod, directs you to an interactive kiosk. It's an engaging check-in experience where you can personalize your visit—choosing room ambience settings from temperature to lighting, right down to the background music. In the waiting area, you're immersed in an environment designed for comfort and education. You instantly notice a refreshment bar—a gesture of hospitality that goes beyond the expected. Here, the receptionist offers a selection of herbal teas and nutritious snacks, transforming the waiting time into a moment of relaxation and nourishment for the body and mind.

In your hands, a tablet becomes a window to new knowledge. With an augmented reality application, you explore health topics in a way that's interactive, immersive, and personalized to your health journey. Posters on the wall spring to life, providing a depth of understanding that pamphlets could never match. Amidst this, a subtle scent fills the air. The receptionist explains it's aromatherapy, intentionally chosen to create an atmosphere of calm. It's a thoughtful touch that eases the inherent tension of waiting for a medical appointment. Instead of outdated magazines, the area features an exhibition of local artists' works. With art therapy books to peruse, the space is transformed into a sanctuary that indulges your senses and promotes healing.

At every turn, the practice has gone above and beyond. Even feedback is revolutionized; with a real-time device, you can express your level of satisfaction, empowering you as a partner in the care experience. The doctor even personally calls to check on your progress, instead of delegating this task to administrative staff. It's a continuous loop of communication, ensuring your comfort is not just met but treasured.

This practice has redefined what it means to stand out, ensuring that from the moment you walk in to the last farewell, your experience is anything but average.

When Details Speak Loudest

In a world brimming with competence (and competition alike), where "good" has become the standard, the nuances of excellence whisper the secrets of distinction. Professionals who stand out are often those who understand that mastery lies not just in grand gestures but also in the eloquence of details. It's the fine print and the subtleties that can amplify a voice in a symphony of sameness.

The same principle applies to the professional imprint you leave. In your look of leadership, it's the attention to detail that speaks volumes. It's the crispness of your white coat; it's the creatively designed name badge that gives away not just your title but also your personal mantra for patient care; it's the well-chosen piece of jewelry, such as a lapel pin in the shape of a medical insignia or a delicate necklace with a charm of the Rod of Asclepius, that subtly announces your dedication to health care.

It's the picture on your website that shows you not just in a sterile environment but surrounded by your entire staff, demonstrating unity and teamwork. This image conveys a message of collaborative care, where every member is valued and plays a crucial role in patient health.

These are the silent yet potent languages of excellence, the dialects of distinction that resonate with both patients and colleagues.

In the same vein, it's the finer details of presentation that can sometimes cause professionals to stand out for, and be remembered for, less favorable reasons, be it a hairstyle more suited to a creative studio than a medical practice, facial hair that ventures into the avant-garde, attire that's too informal or snug, nail art that's more art exhibit than subtle accent, a cloud of overpowering perfume, or an array of jewelry that jangles with every gesture.

It's these memorable yet incongruent details that could lead someone like Dr. Judy to recall an individual not for their professional acumen but for their sartorial choices, thinking, "Ah, yes, that's the person with the strikingly vivid hair color."

Such details, however small and even irrelevant, have the potential to cast a long shadow, sometimes causing the positive aspects of an interaction to fade from memory.

Is this fair? Certainly not. However, humans are built to think this way—this includes you, and it includes me.

Decades ago, I found myself in need of a physical therapist to treat my knee pain. Back then, when the Internet was still a distant dream, I recall the quaint process of selecting a practitioner based solely on insurance coverage and the luck of the draw in a paper telephone directory.

At my appointment, I stumbled into a place that felt more like someone's home than a clinic. I navigated through a cluttered living room adorned with an eclectic assortment of plants, art, and odd collections—a creative chaos, to say the least. Finally, I arrived at the treatment room, painted in sterile mint green, housing one of those physical therapy treatment tables enveloped in disposable paper.

Right there on this paper, which I thought was there for hygienic reasons, my eyes swiftly caught an unexpected sight: the remnants of a chicken bone. You read that right: the remains of what once was supposedly a chicken wing. Despite my initial shock—and I wish I could say I left instantly—I found myself discreetly disposing of the evidence in the therapist's trash can.

Moments later, the therapist entered with a friendly greeting, apologizing briefly for his absence due to a quick lunch break he took between patients.

I don't remember much about the treatment itself. To be fair, it might have been wonderful, his medical analysis might have been on point, and his treatment plan might have made sense. But did I ever return? The answer is no.

Or take the case of my former dentist, who undoubtedly excelled in his dental work. However, every time I reclined in his treatment chair, my attention was drawn to his complexion. It was clear he struggled with severe acne. Now, acne isn't a conscious choice one makes. It's a medical condition influenced by a variety of factors, as you know. Yet despite this understanding, I couldn't help but wonder why my dentist hadn't sought out treatments to alleviate his condition.

Every visit to his office left me grappling with conflicting thoughts. On the one hand, I admired his skill and expertise in dentistry. On the other hand, I couldn't shake the feeling of discomfort caused by the visible signs of his untreated acne. It wasn't that I judged him for his condition; rather, I questioned why someone in his position hadn't taken steps to address it.

Or consider my first-ever therapist, whom I sought out during the pandemic. Our initial consultations, spanning the first half-year, unfolded virtually, with screens serving as our meeting ground. Our conversations provided much-needed support during those trying times. When the opportunity arose to finally meet in-person as the world slowly reopened, we both were eager to see each other face to face.

It was during that first in-person meeting that I couldn't help but notice she was a flagrant nail-biter. Though she didn't engage in the habit in my presence, the telltale signs of its effects were evident. It may seem like a minor detail, one easily overlooked amidst the patience, calmness, and guidance she had provided me with over the screen. Yet from that moment on, I found myself unable to shake the thought: how could someone visibly grappling with such stress and discomfort, evident in the damage inflicted upon her nails, effectively assist me in overcoming the mental challenges I faced?

Now, I'm no medical expert, and I understand there could be various reasons behind her condition. Nonetheless, the visible manifestation of her struggles left me questioning the foundation of our therapeutic relationship. As time passed, I found myself hesitating to return for further sessions, ultimately choosing not to do so without ever articulating the reason why to her.

Successful leaders understand and accept that everything is rooted in the details. Those little details can make us stand out for both the right and the wrong reasons. The challenge is that those details will be of different importance from person to person.

Take, once again, the instances of the chicken bone, the acne, and the nail biting, which may not raise an eyebrow for some patients, but for me, they were enough to influence my perception.

Yet, in contrast, I find myself in the care of a different therapist now. Despite her office being a vibrant collection of eclectic items and her appearance diverging from any conventional expectations, she has a remarkable ability to instantly create an atmosphere of safety, warmth, and comfort. With her, none of those details seem to hold any weight. Every visit leaves me feeling supported, understood, and at ease.

One jarring detail can be enough to get you consigned to the category of loser—or create an unwanted distraction. Within the realm of patient care, it's the myriad of small details that can make a monumental difference in the overall experience. While some of these details may seem trivial at first glance, they possess the power to exert a significant influence on patients' perceptions and satisfaction levels.

Yet despite the challenge of meticulously considering each of these minor aspects, doing so presents a remarkable opportunity for health care professionals to distinguish themselves. In a landscape where many experiences and providers are deemed average, it's these subtle nuances that allow you to stand out—for all the right reasons.

The ABCDEs of Your Professional Imprint

As we piece together the many small interactions we have, a clear picture begins to form. This picture is your professional imprint. Think of it as a puzzle in which each piece, no matter how small, has its own place and reason. Each detail works together to show who you are as a professional. And each element does not exist in isolation; rather, they interlock to form the complete picture that others perceive.

Your professional imprint encompasses a multifaceted blend of choices you make—small or big—that shape how you're perceived and valued in your role.

And this professional imprint is the sum total of your choices in five areas:

- appearance,
- behavior,
- communication,
- digital footprint,
- and environment.

Here's an easy way to remember these five key elements: just think of ABCDE.

YOUR APPEARANCE: Your appearance is your first opportunity to make a statement without saying a word. It's the canvas upon which your personality is painted and the initial impression you leave on others. From the moment someone lays eyes on you, they're subconsciously processing a wealth of information about who you are and what you represent.

Let's start with your body image—the first thing people notice about you. Whether you're tall or short, slim or sturdy, these physical attributes shape the initial perception others form. But it's not just about the shape or size of your body; your overall health, both physical and mental, also radiates through your appearance. A vibrant glow of vitality or a worn-down facade can speak volumes about your well-being.

Clothing is your armor in the battlefield of first impressions. The fit, style, quality, and colors of your attire silently communicate your taste, personality, and attention to detail.

Accessories are the finishing touches that add flair to your ensemble. Whether it's a statement necklace, a sleek watch, or a pair of polished shoes, these embellishments speak volumes about your personality and style.

Maintaining your wardrobe is an often-overlooked aspect of personal presentation. Well-kept garments demonstrate your commitment to professionalism and, again, attention to detail.

Your personal grooming is the final touch that completes your appearance. Skin care, dental hygiene, hair care, and nail maintenance all contribute to your overall presentation.

Your appearance is a silent language that speaks volumes about who you are and how you approach life. It allows you to set the stage for meaningful connections and interactions.

YOUR BEHAVIOR: At the core of your behavior lies your attitude: the vibrant colors that illuminate your outlook on life, ranging from sunny optimism to somber clouds of negativity. Your attitude not only sets the tone for your interactions but also serves as a compass guiding you through life's twists and turns.

Adding depth to your behavior is your charisma (or lack thereof), drawing others into your orbit with your irresistible charm.

Navigating this rich tapestry of behavior requires emotional intelligence: the wisdom to read between the lines and steer gracefully through the intricate labyrinth of human interaction.

But no masterpiece is complete without a sturdy foundation of ethics and morals, the bedrock upon which your character stands firm. And as you navigate the vast canvas of human interaction, diplomacy and courtesy are hopefully your guiding stars.

With your behavior, you not only enhance your effectiveness as a leader but also weave a landscape of lasting relationships and meaningful connections.

YOUR COMMUNICATION: At the heart of communication lies active listening: the art of truly tuning in to others. Through active listening, you not only hear the words spoken but also understand the emotions and intentions behind them.

Adding depth to your communication are your body language and facial expressions, the silent yet eloquent language of gestures, postures, and movements.

Your body and face speak volumes, conveying emotions and attitudes that words alone cannot capture.

And what melody is complete without your voice—the instrument you play every single day? Your voice, with its range of tones, pitches, and cadences. From the gentle lilt of encouragement to the commanding resonance of authority, each vocal element adds depth and richness to your message.

Words themselves are the very essence of communication, and your language palette is the paintbrush with which you craft your message.

Yet it's not just what you say but how you say it that shapes the narrative of your communication. Your communication habits, whether empathetic and concise or passive and manipulative, set the tone for your interactions, guiding the flow of every conversation and shaping the dynamics of relationships. Your accent or dialect may add richness and diversity to these conversations.

Finally, your written communication is the ink that flows through the veins of our interconnected world.

By intentionally weaving together these elements of communication, you create a masterpiece of connection and understanding.

YOUR DIGITAL PRESENCE: Your digital footprint is like a breadcrumb trail scattered across the Internet, each crumb leaving its mark on your online reputation. From intentional actions to those unwittingly left behind, each interaction shapes your digital online persona in the first step, yet your offline persona as a consequence.

At the heart of this trail lies email communication, a digital handshake that speaks volumes about your professionalism and reliability. Similarly, your mobile communication offers glimpses into your accessibility and efficiency.

Venturing into the realm of social media, with your posts, comments, likes, and shares, can enhance your online reputation, positioning you as a credible and insightful voice within your digital community.

In the realm of virtual meetings, your digital footprint takes on a new dimension, showcasing your adaptability and professionalism in remote settings.

Meanwhile, chats and forums serve as arenas for digital discourse, where your contributions reflect your expertise, engagement, credibility, and influence within online communities.

Ultimately, the frequency, savviness, and authenticity of your digital interactions shape your unintentional footprint, influencing how you're perceived in the digital realm.

By actively managing and curating your digital presence, you can craft a compelling online persona that aligns with your professional aspirations and values, leaving a lasting impression on those who encounter your digital trail.

YOUR ENVIRONMENT: Your environment isn't just where you are—it's the vibrant backdrop against which your professional journey unfolds, filled with both tangible and intangible elements that shape your daily experiences and leave an indelible mark on your professional imprint.

Your network, for example, isn't just a list of contacts; it's a living ecosystem that provides support, fosters collaboration, and unlocks doors of opportunity at every turn.

Then there's the spaces you inhabit—the places where you live, work, and everything in between. They're more than just physical locations; they're sanctuaries of productivity, creativity, and inspiration.

And let's not forget about the journey itself: the daily commute, the occasional getaway, and the leisure pursuits that recharge your batteries. From the thrill of exploration to the tranquility of downtime, these experiences add color to the canvas of your professional life, infusing it with excitement, balance, and rejuvenation.

Your environment isn't just a backdrop; it's a character in the story of your professional journey, shaping the plot and influencing the outcome at every twist and turn.

So take a moment to look around. What do you see? How does it make you feel? And most importantly, how can you optimize it to support your goals, reflect your values, and lead you toward success and fulfillment?

Internal and External Consistency

Consistency is the backbone of any credible professional imprint. The key is to ensure your appearance, behavior, communication, digital footprint, and environment all sing the same tune. You can't present yourself as reliable and trustworthy in your clothing, yet behave unpredictably or unprofessionally during interactions. You can't curate an online persona that conflicts with who you are in the real world. Surrounding yourself with luxury and glamour while aspiring to a reputation of humility and service sends mixed messages. Only when all elements of your professional imprint align harmoniously does the message of who you are and what you stand for become unmistakable, compelling, and memorable.

This consistency also extends beyond your personal presentation to maintaining a coherent professional identity both within your institution and in the wider world.

Your *internal* professional imprint pertains to how you present yourself, behave, and communicate within the intricate ecosystem of your health care institution. This encompasses interactions in clinical settings, multidisciplinary team collaborations, consultations with colleagues, and leadership engagements. Colleagues and staff members look up to leaders who demonstrate consistency.

Your *external* professional imprint, in contrast, pertains to how you represent yourself and your institution to external stakeholders, including patients, families, regulatory agencies, or community partners.

Every interaction, whether it's a patient consultation, a public speaking engagement, or a community outreach initiative, shapes the external perception not just of yourself but also of the health care institution and its entire leadership. Consistency in your appearance, behavior, communication, digital presence, and environment internally and externally reinforces trust and credibility, enhancing yours and the institution's reputation.

Yet while this might seem obvious and doable for you, one of the biggest challenges health care leaders face is ensuring consistency not only within their own choices but also among their staff members. Health care is a team-based endeavor in which consistency is essential for the institution's overall perception.

When all staff members consistently follow dress code standards, it creates a sense of unity and professionalism among staff, which can positively impact patient perceptions and overall morale within the team. However, if some staff members exhibit inconsistency in their attire or fail to adhere to grooming standards, it can lead to confusion, discord, and a negative perception within the team and beyond.

When staff members consistently contribute to maintaining a clean, organized, and welcoming workplace, it fosters a sense of pride, professionalism, and accountability among the team. However, inconsistency, such as neglecting to clean shared spaces, failing to address safety hazards promptly, or disregarding infection control protocols, can create tension, discomfort, and dissatisfaction among staff and patients.

Furthermore, when it comes to external consistency, it's crucial for staff members to understand that their appearance, behavior, communication, digital presence, and environment outside the health care institution also reflect upon the institution they represent. And while many staff members may diligently adhere to internal protocols and rules within the confines of the health care institution, there can often be a tendency for some to inadvertently neglect these standards once they step outside the doors.

However, it's crucial for staff to recognize that their choices in public settings directly reflect upon the reputation and credibility of the medical institution they represent—and hence on you.

At any given time, your staff members may encounter patients or community members outside the medical setting. It's crucial they maintain professionalism and discretion in these interactions—anytime, anywhere, with anyone, upholding the reputation of the medical institution they work for.

Your staff members' activities on social media platforms also have a significant impact on the external perception of the medical institution. Even when posting in a personal capacity, they should be mindful of how their online behavior reflects on the institution.

Maintaining internal and external consistency is not solely the responsibility of health care leaders; it extends to every staff member. And if this sounds like a familiar challenge to you, in another chapter of this book, I will delve deeper into strategies and techniques for effectively addressing these challenges with your staff, providing tips and insights to support you in having these kinds of sensitive conversations to ensure you continue to foster a culture of consistency and excellence among everyone—your staff and yourself.

Chapter 3
Leaders Look Confident

Confidence Isn't Thinking You Are Better. It's Realizing You Have No Reason to Compare Yourself.

Chapter 3:
Leaders Look Confident

What is confidence, what does it mean to look confident, and why would it matter for a leader? It's indeed a complex question. Confidence, in the broadest sense, is not merely about possessing a firm belief in one's abilities or the decisions one makes. It transcends the boundaries of self-assurance to encompass an aura of competence, empathy, and unwavering authority that inspires trust, respect, and a sense of security among all stakeholders—be it patients, colleagues, staff, or the wider community. In the fast-paced, high-stakes environment of health care, where decisions often carry the weight of life-altering consequences, the confidence of a leader becomes, in fact, a cornerstone.

Confidence is a complex construct, built from a mosaic of internal and external factors. Your appearance is just one of the elements that contribute, yet it plays a significant role. The "look of confidence" may at first glance seem superficial to some. However, its impact is far-reaching, deeply rooted in the psychological interplay between self-perception and public perception.

The notion to "just dress confidently and others will instantly recognize your confidence" oversimplifies the depth of how confidence is conveyed and perceived. Nonetheless, the visual aspect of leadership acts as a powerful filter through which both the leader and those they lead interpret your confidence (or lack thereof).

Let's first explore the internal dimension of dressing with confidence. It's a universally acknowledged truth that when we look good, we feel good. This isn't a shallow vanity but a reflection of how closely intertwined our self-esteem and self-perception are with our external appearance.

Clothes do more than just cover us up; they can make us feel good or uneasy, especially at work. Researcher *Kim K. P. Johnson* and her team, responsible for the article *Dress, Body and Self: Research on the Social Psychology of Dress*, found that when professionals dressed right for their job, they felt more sure of themselves. They associated psychological discomfort with wearing inappropriate dress for work. *Mary Katherine Brock's* research confirms that young teenage girls' confidence is heavily influenced by the clothes they wear. Even color seems to matter, as *Craig Roberts* and his research team point out, because certain colors, such as red, could boost confidence in individuals.

Lastly, *Hajo Adam and Adam D. Galinsky* introduced the concept of "enclothed cognition," which means what we wear can change the way we think and feel. Their research may particularly hit home for you due to its focus on the significance of wearing white coats. Their study delves into how this attire impacts mental processes. They discovered that wearing a white coat can sharpen a person's focus and carefulness. However, the effect varied based on the described purpose of the coat: white coats labeled as belonging to doctors enhanced attentiveness more than those described as painters' coats. This indicates that the influence of clothing on cognitive function hinges on both the symbolic association and the physical act of wearing the garment, underscoring the concept they term "enclothed cognition."

So all these studies tell us that what we decide to put on every day can really shape how we feel about ourselves and how we interact with others. It's not just about looking good; it's about feeling good too.

In the context of health care leadership, where the stakes are invariably high and the environment can be as demanding as it is unpredictable, the armor of a well considered wardrobe serves not merely as a physical garment but also as a psychological bolster.

For health care professionals, from the scrubs of a surgeon to the business casual attire of a clinic manager, this might mean attire that resonates with professionalism, competence, and authority enhances one's self-assurance.

On the flip side, the external dimension of dressing with confidence is about how you're perceived by others—patients, staff, colleagues, and the broader community. In health care, where trust, credibility, and authority are the currencies of effective leadership, appearance can significantly influence these perceptions.

However, dressing with confidence doesn't entail a one-size-fits-all formula but rather an alignment with the role's expectations and the broader organizational culture. For example, a family physician's choice to wear more casual and approachable attire can make them more relatable to patients, whereas a hospital administrator in professional, well-tailored attire exudes the authority and attention to detail critical for their role.

The interplay between how we see ourselves and how others see us creates a symbiotic relationship in which internal confidence and external perception reinforce each other. This cycle of positive reinforcement between feeling like a leader and being perceived as one underscores the natural extension of confidence through one's appearance.

Leaders Are Confident about Their Body

Let's start our discussion about confidence by ignoring all the things you can buy at a department store or online and focus on the suit you were born with: *your body*.

For health care professionals, who dedicate their lives to promoting health and well-being, this principle of body confidence should resonate not only in the advice they offer to patients but also in the embodiment of their own professional presence.

The very essence of health care work—caring for others in their most vulnerable moments—requires practitioners to exude a sense of confidence and assurance. But how often do you, as health care professionals, apply these principles of care and acceptance to yourself?

A health care professional who is comfortable in their skin commands a presence that is both authoritative and reassuring.

This presence is critical in medical settings, where the confidence conveyed by the medical caregiver can significantly influence patient perceptions, cooperation, and even outcomes. In addition, by embodying confidence in their physical selves, health care leaders can set a powerful example for colleagues, staff, and the community. They can underscore the message that health and well-being are multifaceted (also extending beyond physical health to include mental and emotional dimensions).

Recognizing the body as a fundamental aspect of your identity and a vessel through which you offer care is the first step toward deeper self-confidence. You need to acknowledge your unique characteristics—your strengths and your limitations—and embrace them as integral parts of who you are.

Because truth be told, while there certainly are some tricks when it comes to dressing your body, you'll never be able to fully change the fundamentals: someone short will never be tall, someone overweight will never look skinny. This acceptance is not resignation but a celebration of diversity and your individuality—and your focus should be on your body's health more than on a measurement tape.

However, research does provide insightful correlations between height, weight, and leadership perception. Sylvia Ann Hewlett and her team surveyed more than 4,000 college-educated professionals and senior executives about executive presence. They found that women are judged more critically by their weight, but men are more likely to be judged by their height. Of those surveyed, 16 percent said it's important for men to be tall, compared to just 6 percent for women.

Height is often perceived as a silent herald of leadership. It's associated with authority, confidence, and dominance. But the intrinsic value of leadership is not measured in inches. While height may contribute to first impressions, enduring leadership is built on the foundation of competence, empathy, and integrity. These are qualities that transcend physical dimensions.

And the reality is that height is a fixed attribute, with limited scope for change. Visual strategies such as posture, wardrobe choices, and the strategic use of footwear can subtly influence the perception of height. Yet these are mere accents to the core of leadership presence.

In contrast, weight, particularly in health care, where the promotion of health and wellness is paramount, inevitably becomes intertwined with the credibility of a health care professional. In the general public opinion, weight, unlike height, is subject to change and is often more directly linked to perceptions of health. Here, health care leaders have a dual role: to model a commitment to health and to defy the stereotypes that unfairly equate physical dimensions with professional capabilities.

Bias related to weight manifests in two opposing but equally prejudicial directions: those who are overweight may be perceived as lacking discipline or health consciousness, whereas those who are underweight can be unfairly viewed as being frail or not robust enough to handle the stress and responsibilities of leadership roles. Both of these stereotypes overlook the individual's actual capabilities and contributions.

The research of *Patricia V. Roehling* and her team highlights how obesity affects perceptions of promotability, demonstrating that obese candidates are often seen as less suitable for promotions compared to individuals with other physical conditions. This bias also extends to leadership perceptions, where obese individuals are significantly underrepresented in top positions within Fortune 100 companies. Additionally, studies by *T. L. Brink*, further supported by *Eden B. King*, reveal that obesity can heavily influence views of one's leadership abilities.

Despite the impact of weight on professional perceptions as highlighted by various studies, the most crucial factor is your own relationship with your body weight because it significantly influences your self-confidence. This internal perception of self-worth and assurance can override external biases and shape how you're viewed in leadership and professional capacities. Hence, for those seeking to align their weight with their health goals and professional identity, the options include the following:

Carry your weight with poise and confidence, no matter the number on the scale. Keep in mind, though, that the right fit of clothing can significantly affect how your weight is perceived by yourself and others. Ill-fitting clothes can add pounds or create an unflattering silhouette that distracts from the professional's expertise. Conversely, well-tailored attire can enhance your presence, contributing positively to your confidence and the overall perception.

The key is the strategic selection of clothing that fits impeccably, thus avoiding adding unnecessary bulk or implying a lack of attention to detail—both of which can detract from your professional identity. And ignore any outdated and oversimplified methods of categorizing body shapes or assigning color themes to you.

This advice, while once popular, not only pigeonholes you but also often overlooks the nuances and individuality of each person's personal style. In health care settings, particularly, such advice must be taken with caution due to the practical requirements of clinical attire or uniforms.

Opt to lose or gain weight, yet the focus should be on health rather than solely on aesthetics. Positive changes in weight can lead to a boost in self-esteem and an improvement in how leaders are perceived by others. And as you know firsthand, this process should be undertaken with mindfulness and health as the priority, ensuring the journey toward weight change is sustainable and reflects a genuine commitment to your personal well-being.

Ultimately, the measure of a leader in health care is not taken from the scales or the height chart but from the impact you have: the lives you touch, the teams you inspire, and the service you provide. Height and weight, while observable markers, are merely the superficial metrics of a much more profound equation.

The essence of leadership radiates from a core of integrity, the expanse of expertise, and the elevation of one's goals and visions.

However, if your outward appearance can amplify your inherent confidence, it's a resource worth harnessing. Visual illusions are powerful tools for enhancing this confidence. They're the subtle yet strategic choices we make in our attire that influence perception.

Embracing these visual techniques does not undermine your authenticity; rather, it underscores your self-awareness and the deliberate cultivation of your professional identity. It's not about misrepresentation but about presenting yourself in a manner that reflects your best qualities and intentions. After all, leadership is a performance art, and every leader is both the sculptor and the sculpture of their professional persona.

Leaders Are Confident about Their Age

Age can be another powerful element in shaping perceptions. It's often associated with experience and wisdom on one end and with energy and innovation on the other. It carries a psychological weight, influencing both the self-perception of health care professionals and the expectations of those they serve.

The spectrum of age in health care is broad and diverse. On one side, there is the seasoned practitioner, whose years are seen as a repository of knowledge, a living library of clinical acumen built on decades of observation, learning, and hands-on care. Their age is often equated with a depth of understanding and a steadying hand that can be both comforting and commanding in the face of medical uncertainty.

Conversely, youth in health care is celebrated for its association with agility, both physical and intellectual. Younger professionals often embody the cutting edge of medical technology and practices, bringing with them a pulse of current education and a hunger for progressive approaches to health and healing. Their age is synonymous with a forward momentum, a drive to innovate and push the boundaries of what is medically possible.

Yet these perceived roles of old and young are not without their challenges. The dichotomy can create an internal conflict for health care professionals as they navigate their careers. Those with years of experience may feel pressured to demonstrate continuous relevance in a rapidly evolving field, while the younger generation might strive to establish authority and earn trust in a hierarchy that traditionally venerates tenure.

Each stage of a professional's career brings with it a unique set of perceptions and expectations, internally felt and externally imposed. It's within this complex landscape that health care leaders must find their footing, leveraging the strengths afforded by their age while transcending any limitations it may seem to impose.

Age, much like height and unlike weight, is an immutable number, a marker of time that, contrary to popular belief, has no direct correlation with success. Across the spectrum of history and into the modern day, leaders have emerged at various stages of their lives, showcasing that age is not a determinant of capability. Success in leadership is age-agnostic, instead reliant on the unique value and experience each individual brings to their role.

The key to navigating age is once again embracing it—owning one's years with confidence. This means drawing focus on the richness of your experience, the depth of your knowledge, and the unique value you add to patient care; it means celebrating milestones and using your accumulated wisdom to influence and inspire.

It's human nature to wish to be perceived as younger or older, but a challenge arises when efforts to alter your age's perception lead to inauthenticity. Yes, visual elements can be used to suggest a more youthful or mature image, but these should be approached with moderation.

Excessive attempts, such as dressing overly "age-inappropriate," extreme dieting or fitness regimens that are unsustainable, the use of heavy makeup to conceal natural features, the adoption of fashion trends that do not align with one's personal style or age, or overindulgence in plastic surgery, can convey a lack of confidence in one's natural progression through life—a message particularly conflicting in health care, where authenticity and trust are paramount. These efforts, while aiming to enhance one's appearance, may instead project a sense of insecurity.

When a health care leader resorts to extreme measures to alter their age appearance, it can overshadow their actual competencies and achievements. It's a delicate balance between using visual elements to slightly adjust your age's perception and overstepping into the territory where those elements detract from your authenticity.

Instead, view your age as an asset, not a barrier. Aim to present yourself in a way that highlights your experience and the intrinsic value you bring to your role. Resist succumbing to societal pressures about age. In embracing your years with dignity and self-respect, you set a positive example of aging for your colleagues, staff, and patients. Remember, it's not the number of years in your life that defines its value but rather the quality and impact of those years within the realm of health care that truly matter.

Leaders Are Confident about Their Gender

Gender dynamics play another significant role in leadership perception. Although the field of health care has traditionally been seen as nurturing—a quality often stereotypically associated with women—it also demands authority, a trait frequently attributed to men. However, modern health care is an arena where such gendered stereotypes are continuously challenged and redefined.

Certain areas of health care may present specific gender-related challenges. For instance, specialties such as obstetrics and gynecology have traditionally been female-dominated, potentially leading to biases in patient preference or hiring practices. Conversely, surgical fields have historically seen more male representation, which can affect leadership opportunities and dynamics within those specialties.

Additionally, patient perceptions can influence the dynamics of gender in health care. Some patients may harbor biases, preferring a health care provider of a particular gender for certain treatments or consultations.

And of course, there's always research to manifest or disprove these assumptions. Research on doctor-patient communication styles by *Vivienne Leung* has revealed diverse findings. She and her research team suggest that, in general, female doctors might engage more warmly with patients, involving more positive dialogue and spending longer time in consultations. This aligns with findings that a significant number of patients express a preference for female OB-GYNs, according to researcher *Katherine Buck*.

Although female doctors are often rated as more empathetic communicators, a meta-analysis by *Judith A. Hall* and her team indicated that although there is a difference in patient satisfaction between genders, it's quite minimal.

The evidence points to subtle differences in communication styles between female and male doctors, each with their own merits in patient interactions. The key takeaway is that communication in health care is nuanced, with varying patient preferences and perceptions influencing the dynamics of doctor-patient relationships.

Leaders in health care must navigate these perceptions, ensuring that the quality of care and professionalism are the foremost criteria for evaluation, not the gender of the provider.

There's no doubt that as a woman in health care leadership, you may grapple from time to time with the "double bind" paradox, needing to be caring yet decisive, authoritative yet compassionate. The only way to navigate this is by embracing your gender identity with confidence, showcasing your unique leadership style without feeling the need to conform to traditionally masculine modes of leadership. By cultivating your personal leadership style that harnesses both nurturing and authoritative qualities, you can redefine what it means to lead with influence and integrity within the health care sector.

Similarly, men may face the expectation to downplay nurturing tendencies in favor of assertiveness. From time to time, you may confront societal pressures to exhibit a form of stoic leadership that downplays the softer skills of empathy and caregiving. Yet the most effective leaders understand the strength in vulnerability and the power of emotional connection. Such a shift not only benefits your team and patients but can also challenge and expand the traditional roles and expectations of men in health care, paving the way for empathetic and patient-centered culture.

Nonbinary and transgender leaders in health care often must navigate a world that is still learning to understand and accept gender beyond the binary. Their visibility in leadership roles is itself an act of courage and representation. For nonbinary and transgender professionals, the challenge is often about being seen and respected for their professional capabilities first, without their gender identity overshadowing their skills and contributions. You can lead the change in advocating for policies and practices that recognize and respect gender diversity, serving as a role model for compassionate and inclusive care. By focusing on their professional acumen and advocating for an environment in which all are evaluated on their abilities and contributions, nonbinary and transgender leaders can help ensure that health care is a field defined by the quality of care provided, not by the gender identity of those providing it.

Embracing your gender identity as part of your leadership style is a profound statement of self-confidence and acceptance that sets a powerful example for others. The key lies in being comfortable in your own skin and using your unique experiences to inform and enhance your leadership approach.

At the core of your professional reputation should always be an unwavering commitment to competence and the quality of care you provide. In such an environment, gender becomes one of many aspects of a leader's identity, not a hurdle to overcome but a facet that contributes to a leader's distinct perspective.

Leaders Are Confident about Their Style

Style is not simply about the clothes you wear; it's a broader expression of your identity. A leader's style is an authentic representation of who they are, offering a glimpse into their personality without uttering a single word.

Although it's essential to respect the professional environment and the people within it, there's ample room to weave in distinctive elements that set you apart. The primary concern is striking a balance: your style should never overshadow your competencies but rather complement and enhance your professional narrative.

It's the subtle uniqueness of a custom-tailored suit, the thoughtful choice of a scarf, or the distinctive flair of a classic watch. It's in the carefully selected pin that subtly celebrates a personal achievement, the pattern of a sock peeking out from a trouser hem, or the choice of a vibrant pocket square that adds a pop of color to a classic ensemble. It's the unique frame of one's glasses or colorful shoelaces that reflect an attention to detail.

These elements should not scream for attention but should invite intrigue and respect.

Leaders who master their style understand that going overboard can be counterproductive. It's not about pushing boundaries to the extreme but about pushing them just enough to be intriguing, memorable, and, above all, true to oneself. Your style should not distract; it should fascinate. It should not raise questions; it should assert confidence.

Defining one's personal style is a journey that many find daunting. Unlike choosing a specialty within health care, which is often dictated by passion or talent, style is more nebulous and more personal, and it doesn't come with a clear road map. It's an introspective quest to articulate how you wish to be seen and understood by the world.

The question "What's your style?" can often leave professionals pondering in silence.

Because it's not just about preference in color or fit; it's also about the message you want to send. And this message is rooted in the values you want to project—confidence, approachability, innovation, tradition—and how these are encapsulated in your attire and demeanor.

Only by answering this underlying question can you begin to craft a style narrative that is not only unique but also aligns with your authentic self, which can lead to curating a wardrobe and personal brand that consistently and coherently communicate who you are at your core—both as a person and as a leader in health care.

Chapter 4
Leaders Look Authentic

The Art of Standing Out
While Fitting In,
Without Disappearing.

Chapter 4: Leaders Look Authentic

In terms of defining your authentic "look of leadership," one of the basic notions you can take is to say, "What you see is what you get!" There's nothing worse than someone trying to be something they're not. The harder they try, the more inauthentic and phony they appear.

But what does "authentic" truly mean? "Authenticity" is a term that has garnered much attention and various interpretations, particularly in the context of personal development and leadership. At its core, being authentic means being true to one's own personality, spirit, or character. Yet it's a concept that's far more nuanced than simply "being oneself."

Let me share two uncomfortable truths with you. The first is about the essence of authenticity. It's often touted that being authentic means you don't have to care about conforming to expectations or norms. And this can be misleading.

Many hold the belief that being authentic means you can do, say, or wear whatever you want. This is a dangerous misconception, especially prevalent in the advice of "You do you!"—advice that, admittedly, I have given and received as well.

However, this mentality can lead to a disregard for the professional and social norms that facilitate effective interaction within society. Fully embracing the mantra of "You do you" might mistakenly empower an attitude of carelessness, implying that one doesn't need to take into account the broader context or the expectations of others—because "you don't have to care about anyone or anything, anywhere and at any time."

True authenticity isn't about disregarding the impact of your presence on others; it involves aligning your true self with the environment you're in, without losing the core of who you are.

It's a delicate balance between self-expression and situational awareness.

Secondly, the notion that we each have one "authentic self" is a lie. The reality is that we play numerous roles in life. We're parents, children, friends, neighbors, colleagues, and leaders. Each of these roles demands a different facet of our personality and presentation. To be truly successful, you need to adapt your appearance, behavior, and communication to the context of each role. Imagine interacting with your children in the same way as with your patients, or speaking to your parents as you would to your spouse. Although there may be a consistent thread of core values and beliefs that defines you, the expression of your authenticity will naturally vary depending on the situation.

Authenticity, then, is not about a rigid adherence to a single, unchanging self in all contexts. The focus is on being true to your core values while also possessing the flexibility to navigate different environments effectively.

In leadership, this means finding harmony between your personal identity and your professional persona, ensuring that each role you play is infused with your values. This harmony allows for different versions of authenticity that are considerate of both your own self-expression and the expectations of those around you. It's not about concealing who you are; it is about respectfully acknowledging the part you play in each aspect and role of your life and doing so with sincerity and professionalism.

Like it or not, within the health care industry, just as in broader society, people carry implicit expectations—scripts that are often unspoken yet heavily influence perceptions. Your appearance can confirm or challenge these scripts. In a field where trust and competence are paramount, aligning your appearance with professional expectations isn't about diminishing your authenticity; it requires reflecting your authentic self within the context of your role.

During my keynotes, I present participants with various images of individuals dressed in professional attire. I then pose a question to the audience: Which of these individuals would you entrust with your legal battles, your computer setup, or the education of your children? Again and again, the responses are predictably consistent, underscoring how quickly we form perceptions based on appearance.

My audiences' inner dialogue might go something like this: The sharp lines of that charcoal-gray suit, the impeccable white shirt, and the red tie exude a strategic and commanding presence—that's got to be the lawyer. Right next to that person is someone in smart casual attire—a coat, a light shirt without a tie, and slacks. Clearly, that's the IT expert. Then there's someone in a light, pastel dress that flows softly, the kind that suggests kindness and a nurturing spirit; surely, she's the teacher.

It's these small, deliberate choices in attire that speak to us before a word is uttered, painting a picture of who these individuals might be in their professional worlds while expressing their authentic selves in their roles. So let's examine how you, too, can strategically align your visual presentation with your authentic selves.

Keywords Are the Keys to Authenticity

We all carry mental templates of various professionals, and while these templates might differ in detail, they share certain core attributes.

Regarding the lawyer my audience envisions, his attire isn't chosen for its exceptional or creative flair; rather, it's selected for the messages it conveys: reliability, authority, trustworthiness, and consistency. In the legal profession, the keyword that resonates is "trust," not "creativity." Contrast this with the attire of a creative head of marketing in a multimedia firm or the head of a buying department in a retail company. While still donning a suit, the fabric may be more distinctive, featuring an eclectic pattern and unique style elements. Paired with a vibrant shirt and perhaps a brightly colored bow tie or standout accessories, this look captures the essence of "creativity," the keyword for marketing.

Leaders with a keen sense of style understand that their sartorial choices speak volumes about their professional identity. The most authentic leaders are those who maintain consistency in their attire. Known for either their elegant aesthetic or their inventive appearance, they choose a signature look that not only reflects their personality but also aligns with the keyword they represent.

A nurse in a hospital, for instance, embodies the keyword "care." Her scrubs are not just a uniform; they're a symbol of her dedication and the compassion that is intrinsic to her role. The colors might be soothing, the fit practical, enabling swift movement, and the fabric durable yet comfortable. Every aspect of her attire aligns with the primary function of her profession: providing care. The public expectation is that a nurse's appearance should project a sense of professionalism, cleanliness, and accessibility, all of which are key to establishing immediate trust with patients and their families in the often stressful environment of a hospital.

In contrast, consider a chiropractor in private practice who also embodies the keyword "care." This professional might choose attire that bridges the gap between clinical authority and personal approachability. For instance, they might wear a smart-casual ensemble such as a button-up shirt and slacks. Their choice of clothing is also a deliberate choice to align with the expectations of patients who seek not only medical expertise but also a one-on-one connection with and care from their health care provider.

In both cases, the visual presentation is carefully curated to match the keywords of their professions. It's not a facade but a genuine reflection of their roles and the values they uphold. The nurse's scrubs and the chiropractor's smart-casual attire are not just about meeting the dress code; they're about embodying the essence of their professions and the authentic service they provide.

In every industry, there exists some form of a "uniform"—a sartorial standard that may not be as overt and codified as those of police officers, firefighters, military personnel, or chefs, but it's implicitly understood all the same.

These are the "perceived uniforms," an unspoken dress code shaped by societal expectations and assumptions about certain professions.

The most authentic leaders understand that their appearance is a powerful form of nonverbal communication. Through their chosen style, they convey a narrative about who they are, and they're clear about the keywords that describe this narrative. Each keyword tells a part of your story.

If your professional ethos is grounded in *trust, respect, and loyalty*, your attire should reinforce these qualities. Alternatively, if you pride yourself on being individualistic, fearless, and imaginative, your choices might be more bold and innovative, reflecting a pioneering spirit.

Have you considered the unique traits that define you at work and how they translate into the visual messages you wish to instantly imprint? Reflecting on these defining traits that make you unique in your professional life and how these translate visually is crucial. Doing so allows you to pinpoint a style that not only makes you self-confident but also conveys the key messages you intend to communicate. It's a process critical in shaping not just any personal style but one that resonates with confidence and the professional identity you want to project.

Once your personal keywords are established, the next phase is alignment—by checking if these keywords echo and resonate with the ethos of your profession.

You might then ask: So what are the expected keywords in health care? The answer lies in the collective expectations of all individuals—patients, families, colleagues—who interact with health care professionals. These keywords become the fabric of the perceived uniform in health care. They reflect the attributes that patients and staff alike associate with medical professionalism and competence.

Yet the precise definition of these expectations and keywords can be complex, influenced by a myriad of factors including your specific medical field, the culture of your institution, your geographical location, or the diverse backgrounds of your patients and your staff you interact with daily.

However, in general, from all possible keywords emerge seven categories of perception personas, each symbolizing a specific set of values and attributes that professionals either find themselves in or are often expected to embody. These personas are not just about the clothes worn; they represent the overall image that professionals are anticipated to uphold at work and in interactions.

If you are fortunate, the keywords you have selected to describe your authentic self align with the persona expected in your professional sphere. When there's a match, it can feel like a natural extension of your identity. Conversely, if there's a disconnect, it can manifest as a nagging sense of being out of place, prompting you to question why you feel like you don't quite belong.

The seven personas can be categorized into two distinct types: your primary persona, which forms the core of your identity, and your secondary persona, which complements and enhances the primary one.

Your primary persona is akin to your DNA—it's the bedrock of your identity. It's reflected in the consistent strands of your character, coloring your instinctive choices and the way you inherently engage with the world.

In contrast, your secondary persona is more fluid, sculpted by the ebb and flow of your external experiences, age, education, preferences, or the continuous curve of personal growth. It grants you the flexibility to adapt, to mold your choices to fit the myriad scenarios you encounter throughout your career and life.

While your primary persona remains unaltered, steadfast in its authenticity, your secondary persona acts as a versatile complement. It doesn't overshadow your core; rather, it expands upon it, allowing you a greater spectrum of expression.

Together, they form a cohesive identity that is both true to your essence and attuned to the nuances of your professional environment.

Before we embark on outlining the personas, it's important to recognize that these personas are not rigid classifications. They do more than just categorize us. They influence our perspective on the world, and consequently, these personas are often reflected in our external presentation—the clothes we choose, the hairstyles we adopt, and the accessories we carry, all of which are outward expressions of our inner narrative. Let's get started with the three primary personas that exist.

The Explorer: Approachable and Relaxed

Explorers embody a spirit that is both adventurous and pragmatic, often reflected in a style that prioritizes comfort and practicality. Their wardrobe choices are less about the latest fashion trends and more about the functionality and durability of the garments. Imagine someone whose attire is as ready for an impromptu trek as it is for a casual business meeting: comfortable jeans paired with a resilient T-shirt, perhaps, and sturdy footwear that speaks to a life in motion.

The Explorer's approach to body image is straightforward and unpretentious. Their physique, whether it's conditioned by active pursuits or carries the robustness of a life well lived, is a testament to their experiences rather than a curated image. In their world, the body is less a canvas for fashion and more a vessel for adventure, a mindset that brings a unique confidence and an unbothered attitude toward societal beauty standards.

In their wardrobe, you'll find clothes that serve a purpose: utility jackets with pockets aplenty, fabrics that can withstand the elements, and colors that blend with the natural world. Maintenance is fuss-free, with a preference for clothing that endures the wear and tear of their explorations without demanding meticulous care.

Their accessories, from the sporty watch on their wrist to the backpack slung over their shoulder, are chosen for resilience and utility, echoing the Explorer's readiness for life's spontaneous adventures.

Grooming is efficient, stripping down to the essentials of cleanliness and health, ensuring they're presentable yet not consumed by vanity.

- **Keyword:** comfort
- **Perceived Traits:** active, adventurous, casual, approachable, optimistic, energetic, natural, direct, spontaneous, enthusiastic
- **Perceived Challenges:** disorganized, dull, graceless, mannerless, ordinary, unambitious, unpolished, weak

The Traditionalist: Trustworthy and Reliable

The Traditionalist carries an air of timeless elegance, radiating a commitment to traditions that is instantly recognizable. Their style is not swayed by passing trends but rooted in classic fashion tenets. Picture someone whose every garment and accessory is chosen with a nod to the past yet fits seamlessly into the present: a well-tailored suit that never goes out of style, a silk blouse that echoes decades of grace, or a pair of oxfords polished to a shine.

Their view on body image aligns with this sense of time-honored style. Traditionalists present themselves in a way that speaks of self-care and a polished demeanor, whether they're lean or carry a more robust frame. Their physique is a testament to their dedication to maintaining a look that reflects their values—understated yet undeniably present.

Their wardrobe is a curated collection of garments that transcend seasonal fashions, favoring quality and craftsmanship over novelty. Each piece is maintained with care, ensuring a presentation that is as pristine as it is respectful of their conservative aesthetic.

Accessories and grooming are conservative. Every item, from watches to cuff links, and every routine, from skincare to hairstyling, is an exercise in restrained elegance. The Traditionalist's visual narrative is one of respect for the past, a serene assurance in the present, and an expectation of continuity into the future.

- **Keyword**: values
- **Perceived Traits:** trustworthy, loyal, organized, practical, consistent, dependable, responsible, reliable, conscientious, appropriate
- **Perceived Challenges:** authoritarian, boring, conformist, inflexible, elitist, predictable, reserved, uncreative

The Cosmopolitan: Sophisticated and Eloquent

The Cosmopolitan is a tableau of luxury and refinement, a sartorial symphony in which each element is carefully selected to harmonize with their sophisticated lifestyle. Their wardrobe whispers of luxury. Designer brands and expensive pieces are chosen not just for their aesthetic appeal but also for their ability to convey an air of exclusivity and worldliness.

Their perception of body image is rooted in elegance. The Cosmopolitan views their physique as a canvas for high fashion, with every line and curve thoughtfully draped in fine fabrics. The way they carry themselves—a blend of poise and assurance—complements their impeccable taste in attire.

Their wardrobe maintenance is an extension of their commitment to elegance, with each piece of clothing receiving the care it deserves to ensure it continues to look its best. Accessories are more than mere embellishments; they're statements of quality and design that speak to their discerning tastes. In grooming and makeup, the Cosmopolitan opts for a look that is polished and sophisticated, never overdone. Their approach is methodical.

Every aspect of their appearance, from skin care to the choice of fragrance, is a deliberate step in crafting an image that resonates with the essence of high society.

- **Keyword:** quality
- **Perceived Traits:** distinguished, proper, notable, cultivated, refined, meticulous, discerning, dignified, excellent
- **Perceived Challenges:** arrogant, bossy, calculating, decadent, impersonal, intolerant, stiff, uncaring

Now, remember that there is no "right" or "wrong" type of primary persona. Each persona, be it the Explorer, Traditionalist, or Cosmopolitan, comes with its unique set of strengths and challenges.

Whether you resonate with the unbound spirit of the Explorer, the steadfast resolve of the Traditionalist, or the sophisticated flair of the Cosmopolitan, each brings its distinctive palette of perceived traits and challenges.

If you embody the Explorer persona, your inherent approachability is a tremendous asset in the health care environment. Patients often seek comfort in the relatability and welcoming approaches you bring to the table, making health care less intimidating and more accessible. Yet if you ascend to a high-ranking role in health care administration, where fiscal responsibilities and strategic decision making are paramount, the casualness of the Explorer may clash with traditional expectations.

As a Traditionalist in the health care realm, your embodiment of trust and reliability is your biggest advantage. Patients, staff, and colleagues alike are drawn to the stability and consistency in your approach, fostering an environment in which protocols and traditions are respected and upheld. This trust is invaluable, especially in situations that demand a steady hand. However, the Traditionalist's preference for tried-and-tested methods may occasionally be at odds with the rapid pace of medical innovation. In an industry that constantly evolves with new treatments and technologies, there's a risk of being perceived as not keeping pace with the latest advances.

For the Cosmopolitan in health care leadership, your desire for quality and your sophisticated presence positions you effectively in high-stakes scenarios. Your polished presence can be particularly compelling in executive roles where decisions impact the health care system at large. However, this same sophistication can sometimes be misinterpreted as detached or distant. The challenge lies in ensuring your pursuit of excellence doesn't overshadow the warmth and personal touch that are critical in health care.

Your primary persona is the quintessence of your being, the inherent nature you carry from the cradle to the crescendo of your career. It's the unchanging core that defines your authentic self, and it's not something you should attempt to alter.

A Cosmopolitan attempting to mimic the Explorer's casual demeanor, or an Explorer trying to copy the Traditionalist's formality, will often feel uncomfortable, just like an ill-fitting garment. This incongruence can radiate subtle cues of inauthenticity, leaving others with a sense of dissonance and sensing that something is amiss, even if they can't pinpoint exactly what it is.

Instead, your adaptability comes from your secondary personas—the versatile facets of your identity that you've honed through experience, environment, and personal growth. These are the aspects you can shift and shape to resonate with different people and situations. They enable you to imprint traits and characteristics onto others, facilitating instant connections without sacrificing the integrity of your true self.

Your power to adapt and connect more effectively with others doesn't come from altering your primary persona but from embracing and cultivating your secondary personas. These are the facets of your identity that are more fluid, allowing for personal expression and change over time. The four secondary personas are not about changing who you are but about expanding the ways you can authentically interact with the world.

The Caregiver: Supportive and Nurturing

The Caregiver's style resonates with a delicate finesse, woven with threads of warmth and nurturing care. Their wardrobe is adorned with fine, small patterns and soft fabrics that offer comfort not only to themselves but also to those in their care. Soft colors such as pastels prevail, reflecting their gentle nature and creating an atmosphere of tranquility. Every piece is chosen with intention, from the smooth textures that invite a comforting touch to the subtle details that signal their attentiveness and kindness.

This persona holds a body image that appreciates subtlety and health, finding beauty in the natural and the genuine. Their physical presence is often characterized by an understated grace, with a physique that is maintained not for vanity but for vitality.

Caregivers curate a wardrobe in which every garment is imbued with a sense of softness. They gravitate toward clothing that balances professional expectations with a personal touch. Think blouses with delicate lace trims, cardigans in soothing hues, and dresses or suits that flow with an effortless grace. Their clothing is not just a uniform but a testament to their role as a nurturer, blending professional demands with innate compassion.

The accessories and grooming habits of Caregivers are reflective of their tender approach to life. Jewelry is often minimal, with pieces that carry personal significance or a story worth sharing. Shoes are chosen for comfort but exude a quiet elegance, while grooming is consistent with their overall ethos: thoughtful, reserved, and impeccably maintained.

They approach makeup as an extension of their care, enhancing features with a gentle hand and ensuring their presence is as comforting as the care they provide.

- **Keyword**: care
- **Perceived Traits:** supportive, caring, warm, nurturing, considerate, compassionate, gentle, soft-spoken, receptive, demure
- **Perceived Challenges:** anxious, emotional, dependent, insecure, noncompetitive, naïve, passive, undemanding, hesitant

The Avant-Garde: Individualistic and Creative

The Avant-Garde stands as a testament to creativity and self-expression. Their appearance is a vibrant tapestry of artistic exploration, and their wardrobe is a curated collection in which each piece tells a story of bold experimentation and the breaking of conventional boundaries.

Audacious colors, emerging designers, and unique silhouettes are the hallmarks of their style, a visual feast that reflects a commitment to pushing the limits of fashion.

In terms of body image, the Avant-Garde sees their physique as a medium for artistic display, embracing a spectrum of styles that challenge traditional beauty norms. They wear their confidence as effortlessly as they do their eclectic mix of garments, radiating a presence that turns heads and sparks conversations.

They approach their health with an artful balance, aligning physical activities and mental practices, although sometimes their artistic pursuits may take them off the path of conventional health routines.

The maintenance of their wardrobe is an act of artistic precision, with each garment meticulously cared for—or totally forgotten in between their creative narrative. Accessories, from jewelry to shoes, are not mere adornments but statements of expressive originality, each selected for its distinctive design and ability to captivate and challenge.

Their grooming routines are yet another avenue for creative expression. Makeup is applied not to beautify but to innovate, and hair and nail care transcend the traditional, becoming an extension of their Avant-Garde identity. Every element of their appearance is a deliberate choice, a part of the creative journey they're on, inviting onlookers to witness the living art that is their life.

- **Keyword:** creativity
- **Perceived Traits:** innovative, imaginative, free-spirited, independent, original, unique, unconventional, fearless, impromptu
- **Perceived Challenges:** unrealistic, undisciplined, opinionated, neglectful, inconsistent, disruptive, contrary, awkward

The Glamorous: Magnetic and Extravagant

The Glamorous persona is synonymous with fashion and an innate sense of style that draws all eyes effortlessly. The wardrobe of the Glamorous is a study in opulence, with each piece reflecting a commitment to attention. Envision attire that radiates allure through its very fibers. The Glamorous aesthetic is a deliberate showcase of self through gleaming sequins, reflective sparkles, and a bold color spectrum that dares to combine the intensity of reds, the depth of blacks, and the regality of purples.

Their understanding of body image is intertwined with personal branding; they sculpt their physical presence as a testament to their taste and status. Fitness routines are not just about health but are part of a larger narrative that complements their aesthetic.

In terms of wardrobe maintenance, they exhibit meticulous care, treating each garment as a treasured piece in their collection of finery. Their accessories—from jewelry to shoes, from watches to gadgets—are chosen for their ability to tell a story of attention and to augment their magnetic presence. These items are not mere embellishments but integral parts of a carefully constructed image.

Their grooming routines are rituals in which skin care, hair care, and makeup are approached with the same intention as their fashion choices. The Glamorous see every aspect of their appearance as an opportunity to exude confidence and a sense of allure. This careful curation of their external self is a reflection of a deep-seated belief in the power of appearance to transform and command respect.

- **Keyword:** attraction
- **Perceived Traits:** trendy, stimulating, popular, magnetic, fit, extravagant, daring, attractive, admirable
- **Perceived Challenges:** pompous, one-dimensional, manipulative, insincere, indiscreet, flamboyant, deceitful, artificial

The Dramatic: Strong and Fearless

The Dramatic persona is a striking figure, manifesting a flair for the bold and theatrical in every aspect of their presence. Their wardrobe is a daring ensemble of statement pieces that command attention, echoing the audacity of their character.

A Dramatic's attire is far from mundane, with each garment selected for its capacity to make a powerful impact, much like the dramatic roles they naturally gravitate toward. It's fashion that doesn't just step into the spotlight—it creates its own, ensuring the Dramatic isn't just seen but remembered.

The Dramatic's body image is intertwined with a sense of performance. They view their physique as a platform for showcasing a commanding presence, with an aura that's as impactful as the roles they assume. Confidence is their costume, draped over a physique that's as dynamic as their sartorial choices, making a statement that's as unforgettable as their dramatic flair.

Their wardrobe maintenance is akin to the upkeep of a theater's costume department: meticulous, deliberate, and always with an eye for the extraordinary.

Accessories and grooming are not mere afterthoughts but integral components of the Dramatic individual's expressive repertoire. Each piece of jewelry, each choice of footwear, each stroke of makeup is a deliberate act of self-expression, contributing to the narrative they live and breathe.

In the world of the Dramatic persona, life is a stage, and they're ever the protagonist, with each element of their appearance meticulously crafted to leave a lasting impression of their indelible mark on the world.

- **Keyword**: power
- **Perceived Traits:** strong, intense, charismatic, demanding, bold, commanding, captivating, aloof, severe, spectacular
- **Perceived Challenges:** tough, possessive, intrusive, intense, insensitive, harsh, dominating, cold

Remember, your primary persona forms the core of your professional identity. Your secondary persona allows you to adapt to various roles, whether it's a reassuring presence for a patient or a decisive leader in a crisis. Balancing these personas is key to meeting diverse expectations while staying true to your core values.

Consider the Caregiver, with its inherent warmth and nurturing essence, often viewed as the most adaptable and universally welcoming in the spectrum of personas. Its gentle nature and delicate approach make it an excellent conduit for embodying the traits most desired by patients: empathy, attentiveness, and warmth.

Yet even if your core identity aligns more closely with the Dramatic, this doesn't place you at a disadvantage. It simply means there are moments, such as when you're at the center stage of a medical conference, where the Dramatic's flair can shine, captivating your colleagues with a commanding presence that befits the setting.

The essence of this concept is contextually curating your expression to meet the moment, enhancing your authentic self without losing the essence of who you are.

As you continue on your journey, let this understanding guide you. Embrace your primary persona as well as the qualities of your secondary persona to navigate the myriad expectations you encounter—in your very own, unique and authentic way.

And should you seek to delve deeper into the fabric of your perceived identity, the end of this book provides a gateway. There, you will find a QR code and a link to a perception persona audit available on my website—a free tool designed to offer insights into which primary or secondary persona you are currently embodying or are perceived as.

Chapter 5
Leaders Look Professional

Strategic Moves to Authority:
Positioning for the End Game.

Chapter 5:
Leaders Look Professional

Navigating the shifting sands of what defines "professional" in today's workplace is an intricate dance. Gone are the days when a crisp suit, a starched white shirt, and a conservative tie marked the unspoken uniform of leadership and ambition. Today, the concept of looking professional is a kaleidoscope, reflecting a spectrum of industries, cultures, generations, and individual expressions.

In the past, dress code levels served as a clear-cut guide to professional attire. They were the yardsticks measuring the seriousness, competence, and purpose of a professional. From the elegance of boardroom attire to the relaxed nuances of baseline casual, these levels provided a script for professional presentation. With their unwavering guidelines and unspoken hierarchy, these levels were once the map by which professionals navigated their wardrobes.

Let's briefly revisit them, not as the definitive rule book they once were but as historical markers from which today's fluid fashion landscape evolved.

Dress Code Level 1: Boardroom Attire was the zenith of professional wear, a bastion of formality. Men donned suits in classic hues of black, navy, or charcoal, with white shirts and classic ties. The only footwear accepted were polished oxfords or derbys. For women, a timeless dress or a two-piece suit, a white blouse, and closed-toe pumps constituted the ensemble, with pantyhose as an indispensable companion, irrespective of the season.

Dress Code Level 2: Traditional Business Attire granted more flexibility. Men could introduce pinstripes and hues of blue, while ties and shoes embraced more color. Women found freedom in a spectrum of dresses, suits, and blouse colors and could even venture into the realm of colored pumps.

Dress Code Level 3: Executive Casual ushered in a more relaxed style. Slacks and sports coats emerged for men, and ties could be skipped. Women could express their individuality with vibrant accessories and a variety of fabric choices, and the first whispers of open-toed shoes circulated.

Dress Code Level 4: Mainstream Casual relaxed the reins further. Formal shirts could be traded for casual alternatives, and women could embrace tops and short sleeves. Shoes and accessories could be casual, showcasing your personality.

Dress Code Level 5: Baseline Casual represented the frontier of informality within a professional context, where clean and presentable denim could make a considered appearance. Yet usually this was the level we expressed only in our homes, far removed from the office's formal expectation.

But let's pause now and consider the present. The rules that once dictated professional attire have been blurred by the evolving landscape of the modern workplace. The once rigid frameworks for professional attire have softened, morphing into a more nuanced spectrum of acceptable workwear.

However, the transition toward a more casual wardrobe in many workplaces has introduced a new challenge: whereas the traditional business dress code was meticulously defined, the concept of "casual" remains somehow nebulous and subjective, which often leads to uncertainty and inconsistency.

The integration of diverse cultural norms into the workplace adds another layer of complexity to defining professional or casual dress. With each culture comes a distinct perspective on what constitutes appropriate work attire, which can vary significantly from one to another.

The generational mosaic present in today's workforce further complicates matters. With multiple generations coexisting in the workplace, each brings its own set of attitudes toward self-expression and conformity.

Moreover, the influence of social media and the Internet has democratized fashion and trendsetting, often blurring the lines further.

Finally, the pandemic has undeniably reshaped our perception as well. The shift to remote work and the adoption of screen-to-screen interactions have introduced a level of informality previously unseen in many sectors. The focus has shifted from full business attire to "camera-ready" tops.

These factors, combined with the rise of individualism, suggest the future of attire in the workplace will continue to evolve, prioritizing adaptability and personal expression alongside traditional notions of professionalism. The challenge for today's leaders is to navigate this ever-changing landscape, setting a standard that balances personal authenticity with the expectations of their professional roles.

For health care professionals, it's important to distill the essence of what professional attire means in this context. The traditional dress codes offer a foundation, but the landscape is shifting, and adaptability is key.

For you, this means recognizing the influence of diverse cultural norms, generational perspectives, the democratization of fashion through social media, and the shifts in work environments due to the pandemic. Your attire should be respectful of your field's gravitas, yet flexible enough to meet the modern world's requirements. You must find a common visual language that speaks to the tradition of the profession while embracing the individuality that different generations bring to the table. This means choosing attire that upholds the dignity of the health care profession while allowing space for personal authenticity and adaptability.

Dr. Fuhr, in his insightful foreword, shares a piece of wisdom from his wonderful wife Judy, whom I respect and adore just as much as him: "Dress for the job you want, not for the one you have."

I wholeheartedly agree and would even dare to expand upon this sage advice. Consider not only the next step in your career journey but also your ultimate goal. If your ambition is to one day be the CEO of a hospital, then it is crucial to embody that executive presence from the very moment you step into the institution.

Present yourself in a manner that allows others to see your potential for leadership at the highest level, to recognize the "CEO potential" that you possess. This isn't just about dressing well; it's about consistently aligning your professional identity with the pinnacle of your career aspirations, ensuring that every day is a testament to where you are headed, not just where you currently stand.

From Scrubs to Suits: The Spectrum of Health Care Attire

The ancient wisdom of Hippocrates, who emphasized the importance of physicians' presentation, still resonates today, with attire remaining a significant aspect of patient perception. Studies have consistently highlighted a preference for traditional medical garb, particularly the white coat, in fostering patient confidence and satisfaction. Research led by *Christopher M. Petrilli* reinforces this, with 53 percent of patient respondents considering medical attire crucial, especially formal wear with a white coat, which notably affected their satisfaction with care.

A study led by *Leiko Yonekura* delves deeper, examining responses from patients, students, and physicians alike to various attire styles. The consensus also leans toward white clothing or coats, especially in emergency situations yet also for psychological consultations in informal attire. Interestingly, attire preferences varied with context, age, and geography, indicating a nuanced approach to professional dress in health care.

The respondents reported discomfort with more casual attire, such as shorts and Bermuda shorts, multiple rings, facial piercings, sandals, extravagant hair colors, long hair, heavy makeup, and large earrings, suggesting professional appearance extends beyond clothing choice, encompassing the overall grooming and presentation of health care providers.

In health care, where the stakes are invariably high, the embodiment of professionalism, of course, transcends your attire, impacting every interaction. It hinges on the reassuring touch, the confident yet compassionate delivery of information, and the ability to maintain composure under pressure. Even in the most casual of dress codes, a health care professional's commitment to their role is reflected in their punctuality, their preparedness, and their attention to detail.

However, especially for those in leadership positions, the challenge is to also model and mentor the visual definition of professionalism. This involves guiding teams to understand doing so sets a standard for how the institution is represented in a visual way.

In the multifaceted world of health care, the concept of professional attire spans a spectrum as diverse as the field itself. At one end, there's the crisp precision of uniforms—the quintessential white coats, scrubs that signal readiness for action, and the practicality of non-slip footwear, all of which serve as beacons of trust and expertise.

In private practices, the dress code often shifts to a more personalized touch; practitioners can wear attire that marries comfort with professionalism, reflecting their individual approach to patient care.

On the other end, high-stakes roles in health care administration or pharmaceutical negotiations call for a more conventional business attire, one that communicates authority and the gravitas of multimillion-dollar decisions.

All attire, from the utility of uniforms to the tailored finesse of boardroom attire, tells a unique story of the role and responsibilities it represents within the health care industry.

Uniforms: Traditional Signatures of Health Care Expertise

If you work in an environment that requires you to wear a uniform, you know uniforms are more than mere fabric; they're emblems of trust, hygiene, and expertise. The uniform speaks before the wearer does, conveying a message of assurance and competence. It's a visual shorthand that tells patients, "You're in capable hands."

Uniforms stand not merely as attire but also as emblems of an ethos in which every caregiver, regardless of their role, is a crucial thread in the health care landscape. They are a visual reminder of unity, reinforcing that the journey to healing is a collective endeavor in which each member's contribution is indispensable.

The psychological interplay between uniform and attitude is profound. For the health care professional, donning a uniform might ignite a sense of pride and duty; for the patient, it's a symbol of hope and reassurance.

Uniforms are usually thoughtfully crafted, blending form with function, ensuring that those who wear them can move, act, and respond without restraint. Every pocket, seam, and button is a testament to the practical demands of health care work. Uniforms evolve to meet the diverse needs of various specialties—a sterile scrub for the surgeon, stretchable fabrics for the physical therapist—and each variation speaks to the specificity of the wearer's daily missions.

Uniforms are silent symbols of safety and hygiene, designed to withstand the rigors of sterilization. This is where the uniform transcends its role as apparel and becomes a guardian of health, ensuring that professionals are not just well dressed but also well prepared to maintain the sanctity of their healing spaces.

Moreover, uniforms serve as a canvas for the narrative of a health care institution. The chosen colors, the emblazoned logo—these are not random selections but deliberate branding choices that convey an institution's ethos. They're visual statements of identity, telling patients and the community what the institution stands for and its place within the larger health care ecosystem.

Legal and ethical considerations also weave through the fabric of uniforms. They fulfill mandates that keep the environment safe for patient and practitioner alike, aligning with regulations that are as much about ethics as they are about aesthetics.

And while the uniform suggests conformity, there is a growing appreciation for individual needs within this framework. Adjustments for personal comfort, different body types, and specific circumstances, like pregnancy, reflect an industry sensitive to the individual behind the uniform. It's an acknowledgment that while the mission is shared, the individuals undertaking it are unique.

Thus, uniforms in health care are not a constraint on personality but rather a platform upon which individuality can be subtly expressed. It's in the careful maintenance, the precise fit, the selection of accessories—a pin, a badge, a watch—that professionals articulate their personal story within the collective narrative. The way one carries one's uniform can speak volumes. Uniforms in health care, therefore, are not just about looking the part; they're about being a part of something greater, something that is both profoundly personal and widely communal in its reach.

Beyond Uniforms: Weaving Individuality into Your Attire

For owners of practices or those in non-uniform environments, freedom of dress represents an opportunity to reflect individuality while still adhering to the principles of professionalism. The challenge, then, becomes how to blend personal expression with the expectations of patients and the medical community. The selected attire remains a subtle form of communication, signaling the wearer's role and expertise and the seriousness with which they approach their profession.

In such scenarios, the selection of attire is a delicate balance between personal expression and the unwritten codes of the health care profession.

A practitioner may opt for a white coat that marries traditional respectability with modern design, perhaps featuring a tailored fit or a distinctive collar that differentiates them from others.

Skipping the white coat altogether opens up a new dimension of personal expression while still adhering to the ethos of health care professionalism. In doing so, practitioners can project an image that is both approachable and personal, which can be particularly advantageous in settings that prioritize patient comfort and the human connection.

When the traditional barrier of the white coat is removed, what emerges is a health care provider seen first as an individual, someone with whom patients can relate on a more personal level. This can be especially beneficial in family practices, counseling, or any health care setting in which a more intimate, trust-based relationship is key. The chosen attire in such an environment speaks volumes about the practitioner's philosophy of care—a philosophy that values openness and personal connection.

This approach, however, does not diminish the importance of attire. It merely shifts the focus to other elements of the ensemble that can convey professionalism. Well-chosen garments that are tailored to fit impeccably, constructed from quality fabrics, and selected in a palette that is both soothing and authoritative can convey a strong sense of professionalism. For example, a crisp button-up shirt paired with a sports coat, trousers, or a sleek dress can maintain the professional standard expected in health care while simultaneously offering a warmer, more personable image.

Moreover, forgoing the white coat provides an opportunity to showcase attention to detail in other ways. The use of tasteful and minimalistic jewelry, a refined watch, or even the choice of sophisticated yet practical footwear can signal a conscientious and diligent character. These elements, when harmoniously combined, can create a professional appearance that is both distinctive and reassuring to patients.

The environment of private practice also offers the opportunity to align one's attire with the branding of the practice itself.

The colors, style, and even material of clothing can subtly echo the practice's ethos, whether it be holistic wellness, cutting-edge technology, or community-centered care. It's a chance to use attire as a branding tool, one that consistently and subtly reinforces the identity of the practice to clients.

For instance, a practice that emphasizes holistic health might incorporate earth tones and organic textures into the dress code, sending a message of natural care and well-being. Conversely, a practice at the forefront of medical technology might opt for a sleek, minimalist wardrobe that resonates with the innovative spirit of its services.

Through these choices, attire becomes an extension of the practice's brand narrative every time a patient steps through the door.

Ultimately, the decision to wear or not wear a white coat is more than a fashion statement; it's a strategic choice that can enhance the patient-practitioner interaction.

It's an acknowledgment that although the white coat has its place and its symbolism, the essence of professionalism is not confined to any single piece of attire but is rather a holistic composition of your appearance and the intangible qualities that foster trust and respect in the health care setting.

High-Stakes Style: Dressing for Health Care's Elite Roles

Transitioning to high-stakes environments within health care, such as executive board meetings, fundraising events, or contract negotiations, the sartorial stakes are still high. Here, the gravitas of formal attire is not just recommended but expected. In such echelons of leadership and decision making, clothing becomes your tool for establishing credibility and authority instantly.

When large-scale decisions with significant financial implications are made, the clarity and confidence formal attire conveys is still instrumental.

Formal attire in these high-pressure scenarios serves as a universal language of responsibility, signaling that the wearer is cognizant of the magnitude of the decisions at hand. It's akin to donning armor; a well-tailored suit or a sharp ensemble becomes a symbol of preparedness for the rigors of negotiation and strategic planning.

This is why, for leaders in high-stakes positions, investing in quality, formal attire is investing in their professional persona. It instills confidence not only in themselves but also in the stakeholders they engage with, underlining the message that they are formidable players in the complex and ever-changing health care landscape.

Yet a suit's not just a suit. A study led by *Neil Howlett* explored, for example, the impact of slight modifications in men's clothing on people's perceptions. Participants rated images of a man dressed in either a bespoke (tailor-made) or a regular (off-the-rack) suit. The suits differed only in minor details, and the images were shown without a face for a brief five seconds.

The findings revealed the participants viewed the man more positively in terms of confidence, success, salary, and flexibility when he wore the bespoke suit compared to the regular one. These results underscore the significant influence minor clothing adjustments can have on the impression others form about us.

Does that mean your only option is a custom-made suit or dress? No! But as you climb the professional hierarchy, the imperative for sartorial precision escalates. Your attire is not a superficial layer but an integral part of the leadership narrative you craft. Although a bespoke suit or dress may not be in everyone's reach, the quintessence lies in embodying the role you hold with an impeccable presentation.

The primary point is the meticulousness with which you select and wear your professional attire, reflecting your stature and the seriousness you attribute to your role. Dressing with such intention is less about the cost and more about the commitment to excellence and the nonverbal assertion of your leadership caliber.

Dressing beyond the Code: Situational Awareness

In a world where the white coat symbolizes a blend of scientific rigor and compassionate care, there comes a time when even the most stringent dress codes must yield to the demands of the moment. The true art for health care professionals lies not in the adherence to a specific attire but in the thoughtful adaptation of one's dress to the context at hand.

Consider the times when nature's fury unleashes itself upon communities, and health care professionals become first responders. Their attire is a testament to pragmatism. The fleece jackets worn during relief efforts may not align with traditional dress codes, but they resonate with the immediate needs of the crisis at hand.

Similarly, the COVID-19 pandemic has transformed health care attire into a barrier against contagion, prioritizing function and safety over formality.

But the nuances of attire adjustment extend beyond these extraordinary circumstances. Health care is a multifaceted world in which professionals might trade their scrubs for business casual when attending community health seminars, or perhaps don more formal attire for fundraising galas. In these less dramatic yet significant moments, the ability to modulate one's dress code is crucial. It demands choosing the appropriate attire that aligns with the event's intent, whether it's to educate, advocate, or celebrate within the health care community.

Even outside the clinical or formal settings, health care professionals carry the mantle of their profession. They're woven into the fabric of the communities they serve, often recognized and respected beyond their hospital's or practice's walls. The casual encounters at the local market, the school functions, the neighborhood gatherings—these are all opportunities to present a professional identity, albeit more relaxed. A health care provider's appearance in these settings may not require the formal trappings of their day job, but it should still reflect the respect and dignity of their profession.

As a leader, it's your responsibility and challenge alike to also share this demand with your staff, setting the foundation for their understanding that even outside the medical setting, their professional identity continues to speak volumes, embodying the values and responsibilities of their calling. Their attire becomes also a subtle form of communication. It doesn't need to be the starched uniform that denotes their role when off-duty but rather a mode of dress that balances approachability with propriety and represents the medical institution they work for.

Moreover, the choice of attire in these settings can reinforce the trust the public places in the entire health care profession. It's an opportunity to demonstrate that while you and they may be "off the clock," your commitment to health is a constant.

Ultimately, in every setting, the goal is to dress in a way that respects the esteemed role you play in society. This does not imply a forfeiture of personal style but rather an integration of individual taste with the overarching narrative of your professional ethos. The message is clear: whether in scrubs or street clothes, the individual is a health care professional, dedicated not just during office hours but as an enduring facet of their identity.

Chapter 6
Leaders Look Respectful

Failing to Respect Yourself
Casts Doubt on Your Ability to
Respect Others.

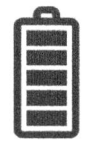

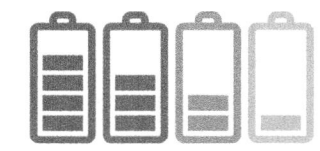

Chapter 6:
Leaders Look Respectful

The concept of respect is foundational in any sphere, and in leadership it's a cornerstone that cannot be overstressed. Respect is the glue that binds together the strands of integrity, credibility, and authority in a leader's tapestry. It's a multifaceted gem reflecting leaders' regard for themselves, their position, their colleagues, their staff, and the collective ethos of the institution they represent.

Respect in the realm of leadership and attire is a silent yet potent communicator. It articulates values and sets a tone for interactions even before a word is spoken. When leaders dress with respect, they make a statement about their personal standards and their commitment to the role they occupy. It's a manifestation of self-regard and an acknowledgment of the mantle of responsibility they carry.

Conversely, a lack of respect in attire can undermine a leader's authority, erode trust, and create an atmosphere of laxity that might influence the entire institution. It can result in diminished morale among team members, a reduction in the leader's influence, and potentially a loss of opportunities for the leader and their institution.

Respect is not a one-way street; it's reciprocal. When leaders show respect for themselves, for example, through their attire, they're more likely to receive respect in return. This mutual respect is essential for creating and maintaining strong, productive relationships within the workplace.

In the realm of health care, respect holds a particularly profound significance, serving as the bedrock upon which the patient-provider relationship is built.

When doctors, nurses, or health care administrators present themselves with a respectful appearance, it's a visual pledge of their dedication to their patients and their craft.

A health care setting is a nexus of vulnerability and hope, where the attire of the staff can either reinforce a therapeutic atmosphere or detract from it. A respectful appearance echoes the solemnity of the healing environment and the gravity of the care provided.

It's an acknowledgment of the trust placed in health care providers by patients who are often at their most fragile. The focus here is on choosing attire that is considerate of the diverse backgrounds and beliefs of the patient population served.

Dressing respectfully is a daily affirmation of your commitment and the high standards to which you hold yourself. Thus, as we segue into the intricate dance between self-respect and respect for others in health care, it becomes clear that respectful attire is a silent yet powerful form of your communication.

It's a Sign of Self-Respect

Self-respect is not a veneer of self-importance but a deep-rooted acknowledgment of one's worth and capabilities. It's manifest in the meticulous care health care professionals take in their appearance, reflecting an inner ethos of precision and attention to detail that is vital in their field.

It's the physician whose attire is impeccable, signaling a respect for the sanctity of their work. It's the nurse whose scrubs are pristine, reflecting an unwavering commitment to hygiene and care. It's the administrator whose polished look underlines the seriousness with which they undertake their responsibilities. Self-respect is evident in the quality of the white coat, the fit of the scrubs, and the choice of accessories that, while subtle, speak volumes.

Dressing with self-respect in health care is not just about the price tag or the brand. Instead, it's choosing attire that fits well, is appropriate for the role, and is maintained with care.

It requires you to understand that while trends come and go, the principles of professionalism remain constant. At the foundation, it's respecting that your wardrobe should be curated with the same precision as you would apply to your work.

This level of self-respect should not ebb away at the end of your shift but should remain a constant in every facet of life. And this armor of self-respect is not about vanity or superficiality; instead, it is about the pride that comes from knowing you've put forth your best self, in every aspect.

Investing in your appearance goes beyond the surface; it should become a daily ritual of preparing yourself to face the challenges and responsibilities of the health care environment. It shows a readiness to serve and an understanding of the gravity of your work. And that might require not just time but also financial investments from your side. This is not to imply that you should spend beyond your means; rather, you should seek the best you can afford within your budget.

Investing in yourself is a nonverbal affirmation of your worth and a visible commitment to excellence. It's a daily reminder to yourself of the importance of the work you do and the respect you owe yourself as a professional.

It also sets a standard because you lead by example and show you value and respect not only your position but also the people you lead.

Leaders who exhibit this level of self-respect inspire confidence and motivate their teams to also take pride in their professional presence. This cyclical reinforcement of respect is what elevates a health care team from merely functioning to excelling in their field.

It Shows That You Respect Others

For health care professionals, showing respect through their attire is not merely a social nicety but a profound acknowledgment of the trust and vulnerability inherent in the patient-caregiver relationship.

The meticulous choice of attire communicates to patients, family members, and caregivers that they're in a place where their health and concerns are taken seriously.

The health care environment is a microcosm of the world at large, brimming with diverse cultures, genders, and generations. Each interaction is a chance to honor these differences through professional dress that conveys respect. By considering cultural sensitivities, avoiding stereotypical assumptions, and choosing appropriate attire, health care professionals show a deep respect for the unique identities and backgrounds of their colleagues and patients.

The key is subtlety and appropriateness. For instance, a pediatrician might choose to wear a cheerful tie or a brooch to put young patients at ease but remain always within the bounds of professional decorum. The attire should be chosen to comfort and reassure, not to overshadow the primary goals of health care: healing and well-being. Similarly, a surgeon's scrubs are a universal symbol of preparedness and expertise, and any deviation from this norm could cause unnecessary concern or doubt in the minds of patients and their families.

Avoiding distraction also means personal grooming choices that accompany one's attire. The goal is to project an image that is not only respectful of others but also reflective of the gravity and precision inherent in the field of health care.

Ultimately, the avoidance of distraction through attire is a health care professional's silent contract with those they serve, promising that their focus is unwavering, their commitment absolute, and their dedication to health and care paramount. It's a delicate balance between personal expression and professional expectation, and striking this balance is an art that every health care leader must master.

Whether it's a storied hospital or your own practice, your appearance should mirror the values and standards of the institution you represent. Your appropriate attire not only respects the institution's image but also its legacy and place in the community.

Finally, how you dress yourself is a testament to your reverence for the industry itself—an industry predicated on the tenets of care, precision, and continuous improvement. Your professional appearance is a nod to the history of health care, a field built upon the shoulders of countless dedicated individuals who have donned their attire with pride. It's a daily, visual oath to uphold the dignity and integrity that are the essence of your noble calling.

Chapter 7
Leaders Look Controlled

The More You Control,
the Better the Outcome.

Chapter 7:
Leaders Look Controlled

Self-control, an attribute as vital to a leader as their ability to strategize or innovate, manifests profoundly in one's professional identity. The tapestry of one's perception is indeed a puzzle, with innumerable pieces that must be meticulously placed with intention and care. It's an art form where the canvas is the self, and every brushstroke is a choice that contributes to the overarching picture of who we are in the eyes of the world.

Consider your image a continuous curation of your professional persona. Every element, from the polish on your shoes to the precision of your haircut, is a testament to the degree of control you exert over your narrative. It can be a narrative that says, "I'm the master of my fate; I'm the captain of my success," without uttering a single word. This silent eloquence speaks volumes about your confidence and the respect you command.

Leaders who grasp the reins of their image do so not by chance but through a disciplined regimen that mirrors their professional routine. They understand that although they cannot control every piece of the puzzle, neglecting to shape their image invites others to fill in the blanks—often with less flattering strokes. The narrative can be hijacked by external interpretations, robbing leaders of their power to influence how they're perceived.

Taking control of your image is, therefore, not a superficial act but a strategic one. It's an acknowledgment that although you cannot dictate every aspect of how you're perceived, you can certainly lay down a strong, unmistakable foundation that aligns with the identity you strive to project.

Why relinquish this power? Why leave to chance what you can craft with intent?

Leaders who stand out are those who recognize their image as a dynamic and potent tool in their leadership arsenal. They dress, they groom, and they carry themselves not just with an eye for aesthetics but with a vision for legacy. They're the ones who take control, not just of their meetings and boardrooms but also of the silent narratives they inspire with their presence.

Although the puzzle of your image has many architects, chief among them must always be yourself. It's a declaration of your commitment to the role you play and an invitation to the world to see you as you see yourself.

Embarking on a journey of professional excellence and leadership, especially within the demanding and dynamic realm of health care, requires more than just expertise in your field. It necessitates a holistic approach to personal and professional development. This pivotal role demands not just commitment to your craft but also a deep dedication to cultivating the aspects of self that directly impact your capability to lead, influence, and inspire.

Like a skilled CEO who strategizes, plans, and executes with precision and foresight, you must fully commit to leveraging every tool at your disposal.

At its core, this is a matter of recognizing that your career is not merely a series of job titles, certifications, and achievements but also a reflection of a deliberate and conscious effort to mold and shape your professional identity. This process involves a continuous cycle of self-awareness and reflection, self-care and discipline, and self-improvement and promotion.

In doing so, you not only elevate your own career but also set a precedent for excellence, integrity, and respect within your field. It's a testament to the fact that being at the helm of your career means fully embracing the responsibility to cultivate an image that resonates with self-respect and the unwavering commitment to serve and lead.

Self-Awareness and Self-Reflection

Self-awareness and self-reflection stand as the cornerstone of professional growth and leadership, particularly within the health care sector. This process begins with a profound understanding of one's strengths, weaknesses, and values and the impact one has on others. It involves a continuous inward journey, asking oneself hard questions about personal and professional motives and biases and the implications of one's choices and actions.

The process encourages a pause after each encounter to consider what went well, what didn't, and how things can be improved. This reflective practice is vital in a field that is as fast-paced and as emotionally charged as health care, providing a means to learn from every situation and to integrate those lessons into future care.

Moreover, self-awareness in health care transcends personal introspection; it extends into understanding how one's professional choices and interpersonal interactions contribute to the larger health care environment. This is rooted in recognizing the role one plays within a team, how leadership styles affect team dynamics, and how one's choices impact patient care and outcomes.

For health care leaders, self-awareness and reflection are indispensable tools in maintaining the delicate balance between authoritative decision making and compassionate care. They enable leaders to navigate the complexities of their roles with empathy, integrity, and a deep sense of responsibility.

By fostering a culture of self-awareness and reflective practice, health care leaders can inspire their teams to strive for excellence, to approach patient care with a blend of scientific rigor and humane consideration, and to continuously seek improvement in both personal and professional realms.

Self-awareness and reflection profoundly influence your "look of leadership," guiding you in crafting an appearance that resonates with your role, values, and the expectations of those you serve.

This introspection allows you to choose attire that aligns with your personal identity while still adhering to the standards and norms of your profession.

Reflecting on your appearance is more than a superficial consideration; you need to recognize how your visual appearance contributes—or doesn't—to perceptions of competence, approachability, and professionalism. A leader who is self-aware knows their appearance can either build bridges or create barriers in these critical relationships.

This includes considering the messages sent by certain styles, colors, fabrics, patterns, or levels of formality. It involves asking yourself questions like "Does my attire convey the authority and expertise expected of my role?" or "Is my appearance accessible and reassuring to patients from diverse backgrounds?" or "How does my personal style affect my team's perception of my leadership?"

Ultimately, the link between self-awareness, reflection, and your "look of leadership" is about consciously choosing an appearance that supports your professional goals, reflects respect for the profession and those it serves, and communicates the qualities essential for effective leadership in health care. Make deliberate choices that reinforce your identity as a leader who is not only competent and knowledgeable but also empathetic and connected to the human experience of health care.

Self-Care and Self-Discipline

Self-care and self-discipline act as twin pillars that support both your personal well-being and professional excellence. At its core, self-care is about nurturing your physical, emotional, and mental health through practices that replenish and revitalize you. It's acknowledging that to serve others effectively, you must first attend to your own needs.

Just as the well known airline safety instruction advises us to secure our own oxygen masks before assisting others, self-care in leadership operates on a similar idea: if you neglect your well-being, it becomes evident in your capacity to lead. It's a simple yet profound principle: to be seen as capable of caring for others, you must visibly care for yourself first.

Self-care isn't an indulgence; it's a fundamental aspect of effective leadership, signaling to those around you that you're equipped to manage not just yourself but also the responsibilities and people entrusted to your leadership and your medical care.

Discipline, on the other hand, is the commitment to maintaining these self-care practices regularly and making choices that align with your long-term goals and values, even when they require sacrifice or delay of gratification. This includes a broad spectrum of habits that keep you at your best—be it through adequate sleep, nutritious eating, physical activity, or mindfulness practices. These activities are not luxuries but necessities that enable you to perform at your peak.

Discipline, especially in the context of self-care, also involves setting boundaries to protect your time and energy. It means being able to say no to nonessential demands and recognizing when you need to step back and recharge. It not only prevents burnout but also models healthy behavior for your staff, reinforcing the importance of well-being in sustaining high performance.

In the realm of health care leadership, self-care and discipline are not just personal virtues; they're professional imperatives that directly impact your appearance and, by extension, your "look of leadership."

As a health care leader, you're a visible symbol of the profession's values. Your disciplined approach to self-care is a testament to your commitment to those values. It demonstrates to your patients, staff, and colleagues that you respect the profession enough to present the best version of yourself.

This doesn't mean perfection or a rigid adherence to unrealistic standards of beauty or fitness. Instead, it is about presenting yourself in a way that shows you take your role seriously and respect the trust placed in you.

Self-Improvement and Self-Promotion

In the dynamic landscape of health care leadership, self-improvement and self-promotion underscore the continuous journey of growth and the strategic showcasing of your capabilities.

As the CEO of your career, embracing self-improvement is about recognizing that the path to leadership excellence is ongoing. It's a commitment to lifelong learning, skill enhancement, and personal development.

Simultaneously, self-promotion, often misunderstood as bragging or boasting, is actually about appropriately communicating your achievements and the value you bring to your role and institution. That requires making your contributions visible and understood, not just for recognition but also to inspire others, advocate for your and your team's work, and contribute to the broader goals of your health care institution.

Self-improvement and self-promotion are intertwined, reflecting a proactive approach to personal and professional development. This approach involves setting clear goals, seeking feedback, and taking concrete steps to enhance your knowledge and skills. This could mean pursuing further education or certifications or engaging in professional networks and conferences.

In terms of your "look of leadership," this means staying informed about the nuances of professional attire within your field, understanding the impact of your visual presentation on patient confidence and team morale. It involves regularly evaluating and updating your wardrobe to ensure it reflects both your role's authority and approachability.

Your choice of attire can serve as a visual curriculum vitae, conveying your dedication, experience, and attention to detail.

Through these efforts, you not only elevate your own standing but also inspire those around you to strive for greater heights, fostering an environment in which image is relevant and encouraged.

Ultimately, your appearance is a powerful tool in the promotion of your professional identity. By dedicating yourself to self-improvement and thoughtful self-promotion, you ensure your look of leadership in health care is one that inspires confidence, respect, and trust, making a profound and positive impact on those around you.

Keeping Control in the Midst of Chaos

In the realm of health care, professionals navigate an environment that is inherently more emotionally charged than many other industries. This unique aspect of the health care sector is a direct consequence of its core mission: to care for human life in its most vulnerable states.

The stakes are high, the scenarios are often critical, and the emotional investment from all parties involved—patients, their caregivers, and health care staff members themselves—is intense and deeply personal. Recognizing and understanding this emotionally charged atmosphere is crucial for you and your staff because it significantly impacts your approach during day-to-day interactions. Leadership that disregards the emotional context comes across as detached or insensitive, eroding trust and morale.

For health care professionals, keeping control in an often uncontrolled world is not just about managing logistics or operational challenges; it hinges on understanding and navigating this emotional landscape consciously—ensuring that nothing distracts from the best possible support of those they serve, especially not staff members' appearance.

Instead of distraction, your attire should whisper instant calmness, competence, and control. And the constant dance between authority and warmth must extend beyond your wardrobe. A warm smile, a direct gaze—these are the unspoken languages of empathy, calm, and care. Your attire is a conversation without words with those you serve. It should be deliberate and considered, chosen with an awareness of the powerful role clothing plays in your profession.

So as you stand in front of your wardrobe each morning, consider the day ahead. You might find yourself in situations where a commanding presence is required, where your attire needs to convey a silent but unmistakable message of leadership and control. But equally, there will be moments where the barriers need to come down, where the soft hues of your jacket, the gentle curve of a blouse collar, or the subtle print of a dress signals a readiness to listen and comfort.

Be Prepared for the Predictable and the Unpredictable

In a world teeming with uncertainty and constant change, the preparedness to face both the predictable and the unpredictable becomes a defining trait of effective leadership, particularly in the health care profession.

As health care professionals, you stand at the confluence of human vulnerability and the relentless pursuit of wellness, a place where the foresight to anticipate needs and the agility to respond to sudden shifts are equally vital.

Your wardrobe, an extension of your professional identity, should be curated not just for aesthetic appeal but for its strategic function. Dressing with intention is an exercise in scenario planning, a rehearsal for the diverse roles you must play to align the tangible elements of your attire with the intangible dynamics of your day.

Embarking on this sartorial strategy requires contemplation—a series of reflective questions that guide your choices and ensure your visual presentation is congruent with your professional objectives. Consider the following:

- What's the big picture for today?
- What's the occasion?
- With whom will you be interacting?
- What will they be wearing?
- What will your client be wearing?
- What will your audience be wearing?

- What will your boss be wearing?
- What will your colleagues be wearing?
- What will your team members be wearing?
- Where are you going to meet?
- Where are you possibly heading after you've met?
- How will you get there?
- Who else could you randomly meet today?
- Which message do you have to deliver today?

The answers to these questions form the blueprint of your appearance. They lead you to select attire that resonates with the contexts you might encounter, clothes that allow you to stand out for the right reasons: precision in your role, empathy in your interactions, and foresight in your readiness for the day's demands.

By preparing for both the predictable and the unpredictable in your professional attire, you assert control over an aspect of your career often left to chance. It's a proactive step toward defining your leadership image—one that says you are as commanding in your appearance as you are in your professional capabilities. This is the armor and wisdom of a health care leader ready to face the day's battles, both seen and unforeseen, with the confidence and respect the role demands.

It's Not Only about Clothes

Yes, looking the part is merely the opening act. It's true that a polished appearance can open doors and instill confidence, but it's the substance behind the style that truly defines a leader. Remember that it's not only about the clothes you wear; it also centers around embodying the values and responsibilities of your role through every aspect of your image.

Your attire might introduce you, but your behavior tells the story of who you truly are. Your communication underscores your competence and empathy, your digital footprint extends your influence beyond the physical walls, and your environment reflects your professional standards.

BEHAVIOR: In the emotionally charged corridors of health care, your behavior carries as much weight as your appearance, if not more. The way you conduct yourself—your actions, reactions, and interactions—becomes a living testament to your leadership and professionalism.

Consider this: you may dress impeccably, with every detail curated to convey authority and care, but if your behavior does not align with this presentation, your appearance becomes an empty shell. In the throes of health care's daily demands, where anxiety and hope often walk hand in hand, your behavior is a beacon guiding those around you. It should embody the virtues your attire suggests.

Your behavior also extends to how you handle the unexpected. In a health care environment, crises are not a matter of *if* but *when*. You might find yourself in the middle of a code blue, where your leadership and decisiveness are crucial. Here, your calm demeanor amidst the storm, your clear commands, and your swift decision making reflect the respect and control suggested by your polished appearance. You must be the calm in the chaos, the clarity in confusion, and the compassion in every care decision you make. Let your behavior be the complement to your attire, not a contradiction—and vice versa.

COMMUNICATION: Effective communication in health care is a nuanced art. It's not merely what you say; it's how you say it. Your tone, your choice of words, and the clarity with which you convey complex medical jargon can alleviate stress or, if mishandled, exacerbate it. Think of it this way: your professional attire opens the door, but your communication invites people in, offering them a seat of comfort in an otherwise intimidating setting.

Imagine you're delivering a diagnosis. Your crisp attire sets a professional tone, but it's your empathetic communication that will be remembered. You choose words that heal, not just inform. You explain; you don't just instruct. You listen—truly listen—not only to respond but also to understand.

In these emotionally charged moments, your ability to communicate with compassion and clarity can make all the difference.

Your communication is the audible manifestation of your leadership. It's a vital component that, when in concert with your appearance, establishes you as a leader who is not only seen but heard and understood.

DIGITAL PRESENCE: Your digital presence is, as you know, also a reflection of your reputation, your expertise, and your judgment. This digital reflection of you can either strengthen trust in your professional capabilities or raise doubts about your appropriateness as a health care provider.

As you navigate the complexities of your digital presence, it's also essential to consider the emotional contexts in which your online persona might be scrutinized. Your digital footprint is not limited to office hours. It's conceivable that while you're immersed in the care of a patient, their loved ones are looking you up online, perhaps in the very waiting room of your practice. They might come across your digital interactions, and this could shape their emotional response before they even meet you.

Furthermore, in the era of telehealth and virtual consultations, the limitations of digital communication become more pronounced. The nuances of body language, the subtleties of facial expressions, and the inflections of your voice are often diminished or distorted through a screen. This can have significant implications for managing patient anxieties and maintaining a calming presence. Your ability to project confidence and empathy, so crucial in face-to-face interactions, must be consciously adapted to maintain the same level of connection in an emotionally charged virtual environment.

ENVIRONMENT: The choices you make in your personal life, from the car you drive to the books on your practice's bookshelves, all contribute to the tapestry of your image. Each decision, even if seemingly unrelated to your professional duties, can nevertheless color the perception others have of you and that they'll gladly misuse, in particular in emotionally charged situations.

Consider, for example, the car you select; it's not just a mode of transport but a statement of your priorities. An outdated, unkempt sedan might inadvertently suggest to some patients a lack of currentness in your medical practice, fostering doubts about your knowledge or resources. Conversely, a flashy sports car might lead to assumptions of extravagance, possibly causing patients to question the costs of their care. It's these nuanced, emotional judgments that could reinforce preexisting notions, particularly in moments where trust and empathy are most needed.

Or think of the people you associate with—friends, family, colleagues. Their appearance, behavior, communication, and digital presence can reflect on you, for better or worse, as well. Remember, you may be judged by the company you keep, so it's wise to surround yourself with individuals who support and enhance your professional identity.

Every aspect of your life contributes to the overarching narrative of who you are as a health care professional and how the assumptions of others either help or hinder you in such an emotionally driven environment.

Chapter 8
Leadership in a Digital Landscape

The More You Share, the More They Discover.
The Less You Share, the More Suspicion You Invite.

Chapter 8:
Leadership in a Digital Landscape

In the vast expanse of the digital landscape, the rules of leadership presentation have undergone a seismic shift. The advent of the Internet, followed by the ubiquity of social media and the increase of virtual encounters, has redefined the parameters. For health care leaders, the pivot from a primarily physical presence to a digital one is not just a transition; it's a transformation that demands an adept understanding of how to navigate this virtual territory.

Gone are the days when the measure of a leader first and foremost was taken through a firm handshake or a look in the eye. Today, it's the digital handshake—be it a LinkedIn profile, a professional bio on a hospital website, or an introductory email—that often precedes any physical meeting. This digital first encounter can be potent enough to influence decisions long before a patient sets foot in your office.

The digital portrait of a health care leader must now be as meticulously curated as their physical appearance. A hastily composed profile, a poorly chosen profile picture, or an unprofessional post can tarnish years of hard-earned respect and authority. It's a world where search engines act as the new background check, and your online persona speaks first, setting the tone for all future interactions.

In this age, it's the digital breadcrumb trail that leads others to your professional doorstep—or doesn't. It forms the narrative of who you are, what you represent, and how you operate within the health care industry. A well managed digital presence can open doors and establish a narrative of expertise and reliability.

Neglect it, and you may find that the narrative is written without your consent, shaped by others' interpretations and the whims of algorithms.

The stakes are indeed high. A leader's digital presence can be the deciding factor in a patient's choice, the clinch in a top recruit's decision to join your team, or the catalyst for a partnership that propels your institution forward.

It has the power to enhance or diminish the hard-earned emblems of your professional standing. As such, it's imperative that health care leaders not only adapt to this digital evolution but also embrace it with the same level of precision and care that they would in any clinical or administrative practice.

In the digital realm, every click, post, and email sent by health care professionals contributes to the *intentional* aspect of their digital footprint. This footprint is a carefully crafted mosaic, each piece a deliberate action adding up to the sum of their online presence. The photograph you choose to display on professional networking sites, the thoughtful articles you publish on patient care, the empathetic comments you leave on forums—these are the brushstrokes of your intentional digital presence.

Yet there's a counterpart to this explicit storytelling: the *unintentional* digital footprint. It's the digital equivalent of body language, the subconscious cues that speak volumes without a single word uttered. This unintentional footprint includes the regularity with which you engage online. Are your posts sporadic or consistent? Do you engage in real-time discourse, or does your silence linger long after a topic has trended?

The state of your professional profiles and website also whispers secrets about your attention to detail and relevance in a rapidly evolving field. A profile with outdated information or a practice website with broken links can inadvertently suggest negligence or a lack of engagement with current trends and technologies.

Your tech-savviness—or lack thereof—reveals itself in the way you navigate digital tools and platforms.

Do you leverage the latest telehealth features to enhance patient care, or do you struggle with the basics of a virtual consultation setup? And let's not forget the omnipotent algorithms of search engines. Your visibility or invisibility on the sought-after first page of Google search results can influence perceived credibility and authority, painting a picture of prominence or obscurity.

In the health care profession, where trust and expertise are paramount, both the intentional and unintentional aspects of your digital footprint must be managed with care. The silent symphony of actions and inactions forms the backdrop against which your explicit digital decisions are set. It's this combination of the overt and the subtle that collectively composes the full digital score of a health care leader's online presence.

KNOW: Assessing the Scope of Your e-Shadow

The first step in managing your digital footprint is simply to know and understand what's currently out there about you. This initial phase requires a comprehensive analysis of your online presence, utilizing search engines and social media platforms, to get an unfiltered view of how you appear to the outside world.

Engage in a methodical search of your name, including the most common typos, and your titles, supplemented by your profession, the name of your practice, or the health care institutions you're connected with, spanning across all search engines such as Google, Bing, and Yahoo to ensure no stone is left unturned.

This step lays bare the expanse of your online presence, revealing everything from professional accomplishments to personal snippets that have made their way onto the digital stage.

To gain an unfiltered perspective of how the digital world perceives you, use incognito or private browsing modes that are features available in most web browsers. This approach strips away the personalization of search results, offering a clear, unfiltered view of your digital footprint as seen through the eyes of someone encountering you for the first time online.

This step ensures you're not just seeing a reflection colored by your own online behavior but the raw, unadulterated image presented to the wider world.

Then continue with social media platforms. Begin with a critical assessment of your profile, profile pictures, and background images across platforms. These visual elements serve as the digital façade of your persona; they're often the first impression someone gets of you online—without reading a word about you. Ensure these images are not just professionally appropriate but also convey a sense of your commitment to health care, whether through imagery related to your field or a simple, dignified portrait that speaks of reliability and trust.

Next, turn your attention to your handles and bio descriptions, as well as the content you've shared. This includes posts, articles, comments, and even likes. Each piece of content should be reflective of your professional values, showcasing your knowledge, your dedication to patient care, and your engagement with the broader health care community. It's not just about avoiding potential pitfalls like controversial statements or unprofessional behavior; it's also about actively contributing to discussions and sharing insights that reinforce your role as a thought leader and a trusted health care provider.

Equally important is the examination of your connections. Remember, the company you keep can influence perceptions of your professional judgment and affiliations. And that is, of course, also true online. Ensure your network is composed only of trusted friends and of colleagues, industry leaders, and institutions that are respected within the health care sector. As a side effect, this not only enhances your professional identity but also enriches your feed with relevant, up-to-date information, keeping you informed and engaged with the latest in health care.

Continue with your virtual meetings setup. For health care professionals, these digital gatherings are not just a matter of convenience but a critical component of patient care and interdepartmental coordination. As such, ensuring a professional appearance and environment during virtual meetings is just as crucial as in-person interactions. Consider the visual backdrop of your virtual meetings. A cluttered background can detract from the meeting's focus and diminish your perceived professionalism. Poor lighting can obscure your face, making communication less effective and diminishing the personal connection that is vital in health care interactions. Audio quality is another critical aspect. Background noise can disrupt the flow of conversation and hinder clear communication. Use a high-quality microphone and consider wearing headphones to minimize external noise.

In the digital era, written communication forms the backbone of daily interactions. Beyond emails and text messages, health care professionals engage in a myriad of digital correspondences, including electronic health records notes, patient portal communications, professional forums, and even comments on relevant online articles or blogs. Each platform and message carries the weight of your professional identity and requires careful consideration.

And always keep in mind that in the interconnected world of digital communication, the reach and permanence of your clicks and words extend far beyond the immediate recipient. Health care professionals especially, who are often entrusted with sensitive information, must be particularly vigilant about the potential for their communications to travel unexpectedly.

Emails can easily be forwarded, and a message crafted for a specific individual or group can quickly find its way into unintended inboxes. Social media posts, despite the illusion of control through privacy settings or the ability to delete, carry the risk of being screenshotted and archived. Once shared publicly, or even with a restricted audience, there's no guarantee against content being captured and redistributed by others. Even virtual meetings introduce the risk of being recorded without explicit consent. Third-party tools can capture audio and visual feeds, making any shared information, casual remarks, or confidential discussions vulnerable to unauthorized distribution.

REPAIR: Correcting Your Cyber Image

This stage involves active measures to amend or mitigate any negative aspects of your online presence—the "obvious problems." Whether it's unflattering comments, outdated images, misleading information, or more egregious issues like unfounded allegations or the unauthorized release of sensitive data, taking decisive action is crucial for upholding your professional integrity.

When the negative content falls within your realm of control, such as your personal or professional social media profiles, websites, or blogs, addressing these issues can be relatively straightforward. This might involve removing or editing the content in question or updating profile details to reflect your current professional status.

The challenge escalates when the adverse content resides outside your direct control, on platforms or websites you do not own. In these cases, the first approach is to directly contact the administrators or creators of the content, courteously requesting its removal or alteration. Clearly explain the negative impact of the content on your professional identity.

If direct appeals are unsuccessful, or if the content's removal is complicated, enlisting the help of reputation management professionals might be necessary. These specialists are adept at devising strategies to remove negative content in search engine results, effectively making it less visible or discoverable to those searching for you online.

Yet during this phase, you should also address the "not so obvious" problems. These are instances where the search results about you don't necessarily cast a negative light, yet they fail to highlight your achievements or expertise or the positive attributes you wish to convey. A search result that doesn't outright damage your reputation but fails to showcase your qualifications or contributions to health care or the values you stand for can be just as detrimental.

The strategy here is twofold: enhancement and creation. Begin by enhancing existing content.

You might even have to reach out to administrators or creators once again, suggesting updates or additions that better represent your professional stature.

Simultaneously, focus on creating new content that accurately reflects your professional identity as a health care leader. This can include publishing articles on reputable health care blogs, participating in interviews or podcasts relevant to your field, or engaging in community health initiatives that garner positive media attention. Leveraging social media platforms to share insights, join professional discussions, and highlight your contributions can also significantly improve the quality of your digital footprint.

Shaping the narrative around your digital presence is crucial. Not only does it ensure that your online persona accurately reflects your real-world expertise and values but it also positions you as a thought leader in your field. This proactive approach ensures that when patients, colleagues, or potential employers search for you online, they will find a comprehensive and positive representation of your professional identity.

OWN: Claiming Your Virtual Real Estate

To address a potential problem, owning your name online is not just a matter of personal branding; it's a strategic necessity. The potential challenge arises when individuals share your name, a scenario not uncommon. From celebrities dominating search engine results to name twins with a more active online presence, these situations can dilute your digital identity, making it harder for patients, colleagues, and industry peers to find the real you.

To navigate this, it's essential to carve out a distinct online presence that unmistakably identifies you. This might mean incorporating your middle name or initials in your professional profiles, using professional titles or abbreviations (e.g., Dr., MD, RN), or adopting a unique variation of your name that's closely tied to your health care specialty.

These modifications ensure that when someone searches for you online, they will find you, not someone else.

Moreover, this strategy serves as a preventive measure against future challenges. The Internet's dynamic nature means that new personalities can emerge overnight, potentially overshadowing your digital presence.

For instance, a new pop star sharing your name could suddenly dominate search results or, worse, someone with a negative reputation could tarnish the name you share. By establishing a clear and unique online identity, you mitigate these risks, ensuring your professional achievements and contributions remain front and center.

This means going beyond merely setting up profiles on popular platforms like LinkedIn or Instagram. It involves a comprehensive approach to claiming your name across all digital channels, ensuring that you, and only you, control how your name is represented online.

The process begins with registering your name on as many social media platforms, professional directories, and relevant online forums as possible. Although it might seem daunting to maintain active profiles on each, the goal isn't necessarily to be active everywhere but to prevent others from assuming your identity or diluting your online presence. By owning your name on these platforms, you create a protective barrier around your digital identity, making it harder for others to impersonate you or misrepresent your professional brand.

Furthermore, secure your domain name (e.g., YourName.com). Even if you don't plan to launch a website immediately, owning your domain name is a vital step in controlling your digital presence. It prevents others from using your name for their purposes and provides a centralized hub for your professional portfolio, accolades, and contributions to health care.

Additionally, explore niche platforms and professional directories specific to the health care industry. These spaces not only allow you to claim your name in more targeted circles but also enhance your visibility among colleagues.

They serve as additional layers of authentication for your professional identity, reinforcing your presence in the health care community.

Taking these proactive steps to own your name across the Internet ensures that when someone searches for you online, they will find a cohesive and controlled narrative that you've curated and that will be seen not just by your patients, staff, and colleagues but also by the broader health care community.

CONTROL: Commanding Your Digital Boundaries

Taking control in the digital realm extends beyond just owning your name across various platforms; it's also about meticulously managing the nuances of your online presence.

First, examine the privacy settings on all your social media profiles. Each platform offers a range of options that control who can see your posts, who can tag you, who can comment on or share your content, and even who can send you friend requests or follow you. It's essential to tailor these settings to suit your personal preferences as well as your professional needs, ensuring your content is visible to the right audience while protecting your privacy.

Also consider the implications of your current connections because they can reflect on your professional persona. Be mindful of whom you accept or seek out because these connections can be viewed as an endorsement of your professional standards and network.

Moreover, be proactive in managing the content associated with your profile. Regularly review tags and mentions, removing or disassociating yourself from any content that doesn't align with your professional identity or privacy preferences. This might include untagging yourself from photos or asking colleagues to refrain from mentioning you in certain posts.

Additionally, think about the visibility of your likes, comments, and shares. These actions can be as telling as the content you post directly.

They contribute to the overall narrative of your professional persona online, so it's wise to conduct these interactions with the same care and consideration you'd give to your own posts.

Finally, keep abreast of updates to privacy policies and settings on each platform. Social media sites frequently update their privacy features, and staying informed allows you to adjust your settings proactively, ensuring continuous control over your digital presence.

By taking these steps, you not only protect your professional reputation but also establish boundaries that respect your privacy and the privacy of those you interact with online. In an era where digital interactions can have real-world implications, such control is not just advisable—it's indispensable.

MONITOR: Persistent Surveillance of Your Online Self

The final step in managing your digital footprint is to vigilantly monitor your online presence. Regularly checking how you appear on the Internet isn't an act of vanity; it's a critical component of professional reputation management. There's no harm and no shame in frequently searching for your name in search engines.

One effective strategy is to set up automated alerts. Most search engines offer this feature for free, sending you notifications whenever your name appears online. This proactive approach ensures you're always informed about your digital mentions, allowing you to address any new content quickly.

Patient reviews and testimonials on search engines, social media platforms, general review sites, or special medical review platforms should be considered too. Thanking patients for positive reviews publicly reinforces the positive aspects of your practice and encourages others to share their experiences.

Conversely, addressing critical comments is just as important. Responding promptly and constructively to negative feedback shows you value patient input and are committed to improving your service.

It's an opportunity to turn a potentially negative situation into a positive demonstration of your dedication to patient care.

In the fast-paced digital world, narratives can quickly spiral out of control if not addressed promptly. Being aware of what's being said about you online allows you to take timely action, whether it's correcting inaccuracies, responding to feedback, or updating your digital content to better reflect your professional identity.

And while it straddles a fine line in terms of privacy, keeping an eye on the digital activities of your staff members can also be prudent.

Whether it's through email communication, virtual meetings, or interactions on various digital platforms, each digital touchpoint offers an opportunity for you to reinforce your professional identity. It's not enough to curate a strong social media presence or a polished professional website; every digital interaction must be approached with the same level of care and strategic thinking.

By applying these steps across all digital mediums, you ensure a cohesive and controlled digital identity. This holistic approach to managing your digital identity not only safeguards your professional reputation but also amplifies the positive impact you can have within your field.

Chapter 9
Leader Lead by Example

By Changing Nothing,
Nothing Changes.

Chapter 9:
Leaders Lead by Example

Your most paramount duty in your leadership role is not just to lead; it's also about cultivating more leaders—by demonstrating that exceptional leadership is less about dictating actions and more about setting a compelling example. By embodying the values and standards you wish to see, you become a leader others are inspired to follow. This approach is what distinguishes a true leader from a mere manager. Whereas managers focus on ensuring tasks are completed, issuing directives, and adhering to the letter of the law, leaders inspire action through their own choices. They don't just tell their team what to do; they show them how it's done. Your actions send a powerful message of "Do as I do," fostering an environment of mutual respect and emulation.

Great leaders intuitively understand that leading by example is the most potent form of guidance that creates an unspoken standard: an organic dress code, a blueprint for behavior, a benchmark for communication, a template for digital engagement, a standard for the living and nonliving elements that you surround yourself with in your environment that is far more influential than any written policy.

Your staff and colleagues are always observing, learning, and, in many cases, emulating your actions. Being a leader means accepting that you're always on stage, setting an example for every person you interact with. And while it might sound obvious, every moment of the day it's crucial, then, to ensure that the example you're setting is a positive one. By practicing what you preach and paying attention to the minutiae of your professional identity, you not only enhance your leadership but also inspire your team to strive for the same excellence.

The flip side, being a poor role model, is the easiest way to undermine your own authority as a leader. Does that mean you have to follow all the rules (and burdens) your institution puts on you? Maybe. Does that mean you can't have your own style, and you can't stand out and show your personality? Absolutely not.

Influential leaders are confident, and they trust themselves enough to live their own interpretation of a professional identity. They've put so much thought into it and created such a defined image that their presence is instantly felt when they walk into the room. They're mindful of how others could perceive them and of how they want to be perceived by others.

If part of this image building requires them to wear denims, they wear denims. If wearing sneakers with their suit adds something unique to their defined image, they wear sneakers. Influential leaders exude confidence and trust in their ability to craft a distinct professional identity that resonates with who they are.

This identity is a reflection of a well considered personal brand that these leaders have meticulously developed over time. Their presence commands attention, not because of what they wear but because of the deliberate thought process behind each choice.

Courageous leaders don't make excuses. They apologize when they've done something wrong. And usually people have the most respect for those who don't hesitate to say, "I'm sorry," or simply "I was wrong."

But people have a hard time respecting those who look for excuses in advance. A leader makes commitments, not excuses. If staff members see commitment, courage, and taking responsibility for the actions and choices leaders have made, it feels safe and right to them to follow that person.

Sometimes professionals claim it's too hot or too cold to dress appropriately, letting the climate dictate their professional standards. Financial concerns also play a role, with some feeling the pinch of investing in high-quality attire, worrying about the cost or grappling with guilt over spending.

Time, that ever-elusive commodity, is another barrier, with the hustle of daily life supposedly leaving little room for meticulous planning.

Amid these justifications, a deeper thread of resistance emerges. Some professionals feel their current look "still works" for them, clinging to a style that may no longer serve their evolving role. A claimed lack of style sense becomes a shield against change, while the actions of colleagues—"They do it too"—serve as misguided validation.

Geographic excuses, like the claim that "We're in the suburbs, not Manhattan," highlight a misunderstanding that professionalism has a zip code.

Venturing into the digital realm, some diminish the importance of a polished online presence with a wave of the hand, dismissing it as "just the Internet." This underestimation overlooks the profound impact of digital impressions in today's interconnected world.

These excuses, while varied, share a common theme: a reluctance to embrace the full spectrum of leadership, which includes presenting oneself in the best possible way. Influential leaders recognize that professionalism isn't confined to a specific weather forecast, price tag, or zip code. It's a commitment to embodying the principles of leadership. This commitment, regardless of external factors, underscores a leader's dedication to their role, their team, and their personal and professional growth.

And it's not just leaders who might find themselves entangled in a web of excuses; these justifications echo through the corridors, whispered by staff at all levels. The reasons for an unprofessional appearance, inappropriate behavior, lax communication, an unfiltered digital footprint, or disorder in their environment are manifold and, at times, mirror those of their leaders. They cite the weather's discomfort or the financial strain of maintaining a professional identity. Time constraints become a convenient scapegoat, with the daily grind supposedly leaving little room for attention to detail.

The narrative extends into the realm of personal expression, where some staff members cling to the idea that their current style suffices, fearing that a more polished appearance, for example, might strip them of their individuality. They observe their colleagues seeking loopholes in the dress code that might justify their choices. Some might downplay the significance of their online image, dismissing it as inconsequential to their real-world responsibilities.

In this landscape of justifications and rationalizations, the role of a leader becomes even more crucial. Successful leaders sidestep these excuses to send a clear message to their staff: professionalism is non-negotiable, integral to the fabric of the institution, and essential for individual and collective success.

The Leader's Challenge: It's Not You, It's Someone Else

Sending a clear message to staff sometimes means having honest conversations with your staff about sensitive topics that can range from inappropriate attire to personal hygiene issues, from mismanagement of emotions to unfortunate social media posts, from neglecting workspaces to disrespecting stakeholders.

Although these discussions may feel uncomfortable, they're integral to maintaining the professional integrity the health care field demands. And it's not uncommon for leaders to feel apprehensive about raising such subjects. Do you? Maybe because . . .

- You aim to foster positive relationships within your staff, knowing harmony is key to effective patient care.

- The thought of causing emotional discomfort to a staff member goes against your instincts as a caregiver.

- Anticipating a negative reaction can be worrisome because it might affect the dynamics of your closely knit staff.

- Asserting authority without coming off as confrontational is crucial to maintaining a collaborative atmosphere.

- Conflict, especially in a setting focused on healing and care, can seem particularly counterintuitive to you.

- Avoiding awkwardness is natural, especially when you spend significant time together focusing on patient well-being.

- Finding the right words to express your concerns can be challenging.

However, remember that first and foremost, your goal is to support your staff members' professional development, not to criticize them personally. Here's how you can approach these delicate conversations with confidence and clarity:

Begin by thoroughly preparing for the discussion. It's crucial to enter these conversations with a clear understanding of the issue at hand. Start by identifying the problem with precision. Reflect on the consequences this problem creates, not just for the individual involved but for the entire team, patients, and the health care environment as a whole. If it doesn't affect anyone, there's no need for a conversation.

Determine who is directly responsible for the issue. It's essential to pinpoint when the issue first arose and assess its frequency. Reflect on previous attempts to address the problem and their outcomes. This preparation helps you approach the conversation with a solid foundation, making it easier to discuss potential solutions effectively.

Finally, assess whether this is a conversation you should have independently or if it would benefit from the presence of another party, such as a human resources representative or a senior colleague. This decision should be based on the nature of the issue, its sensitivity, and the potential impact on the individual or team.

Get guidance before you approach. In any case, it's recommended you consult with human resources or a legal advisor if you have access to such a source, because some issues carry legal implications and require a delicate approach. Before diving into conversations about sensitive topics such as alcohol, drugs, religion, sex, violence, theft, fraud, harassment, or bullying, it's wise to consult with an expert. These experts can provide essential guidance on handling the situation correctly, inform you about any disciplinary actions that may be appropriate, and ensure you adhere to laws and policies.

Seeking such advice serves as a protective measure for both you and your institution. It helps prevent potential missteps that could lead to false accusations or lawsuits. Addressing such matters without proper preparation and understanding of the legal context could inadvertently cause significant harm.

Pick the best time and space. Selecting the appropriate setting for such a delicate conversation is critical, especially within the bustling environment of a hospital or medical practice. These kinds of conversations should never occur in public spaces like hallways, where there's a risk of being overheard or observed by others, compromising the privacy and dignity of the staff member involved.

Instead, opt for a quiet, private space where confidentiality can be maintained—perhaps an office or a secluded meeting room. This environment ensures both you and the staff member feel secure, don't get distracted, and are able to speak openly without fear of interruptions.

Additionally, choosing the right moment can significantly impact the receptiveness and outcome of the discussion. Avoid scheduling these talks during peak operational hours or just before or after stressful procedures or meetings, because stress levels and distractions can hinder the effectiveness of your message.

Instead, find a time when both you and the staff member are least likely to be under immediate pressure, allowing for a more focused, calm, and constructive exchange. Also, you don't want to have to rush through this conversation because doing so could lead to misunderstandings or the feeling that the issue isn't really being taken seriously.

Bring yourself into the right mindset. Remember that these conversations are not personal attacks against your staff member. Instead, they're meant to be constructive and help your staff member, team, and institution improve.

Also, remember that neither of you is probably looking forward to this conversation. It's likely your staff member is just as anxious as you are. So take a few minutes to clear your head and remind yourself of that objective.

Start the conversation with positive reinforcement. This instantly reaffirms the value of your staff member, especially if you share praise about measurable achievements. For health care professionals, this could include citing specific instances in which their attention to detail improved patient outcomes, their quick thinking averted a potential crisis, or their dedication led to a significant reduction in patient recovery times.

Conversely, vague compliments like "You're doing great" or "We appreciate your hard work" lack the specificity needed to make the individual feel genuinely recognized. Such statements, while well intentioned, fail to highlight the unique contributions of the staff member and can, in the end, turn against you: "Well, you said I'm doing great. So what's the point?"

Focusing on concrete achievements sets a constructive tone, demonstrating you value their contributions in a specific area while allowing there is room for improvement in another.

Use neutral and straightforward language. When addressing concerns, it's crucial to be clear and precise to ensure there's no room for misunderstanding. For instance, instead of saying, "You're not engaging enough with patients," you need to specify, "I've observed that during rounds, there are missed opportunities to clearly explain treatment plans to patients." This approach makes your feedback not only more actionable but also less personal and more focused on professional development.

Aim for a delivery that is straightforward and unembellished, yet sensitive. Let the facts speak for themselves, and calmly present them without the distortion of emotional undercurrents. This ensures feedback is received as intended: as a means to improve professional practice and, ultimately, patient care, rather than as a personal critique.

Don't refer to others. When you need to address a concern with a staff member, center the conversation on your own observations and experiences rather than on third-party comments or hearsays. It's crucial to base your conversation on incidents you've witnessed personally, not on anecdotes or grievances passed on by others. If the situation occurred in your absence or cannot be personally verified, it's vital to have written, verifiable evidence to substantiate your points. This approach not only preserves the dignity of your staff but also strengthens the trust between you and them.

Describe the consequences for them and your institution. Articulate the impact on their own reputation and the broader impact of their actions. For instance, explain how their behavior not only hampers their own professional growth but also tarnishes the collective reputation of the team, department, and institution. This perspective shift helps the staff member understand the gravity of the situation beyond their individual sphere. For example, constant tardiness might not only affect their workload but also strain team dynamics and departmental efficiency, potentially compromising the quality of patient care.

However, address these concerns without making it about your personal grievances ("I" statements). The focus should remain on the consequences of their actions on themselves and the institution, not on you as an individual leader. This ensures the feedback is purposeful and targeted toward fostering an environment in which their own well-being and the highest levels of patient care and institutional integrity are maintained.

Be clear about how you would like them to change. Rather than dwell on the past, move quickly on to the future. But don't expect your staff member to know exactly what you expect them to change. For instance, if a staff member has been inconsistent in following hygiene protocols, don't just highlight past oversights. Instead, clearly outline the steps for improvement, such as adhering to a checklist of hygiene practices before and after patient interactions. If your staff member showed up with inappropriate attire, explain exactly what's understood and expected as professional attire.

Specify that these measures are nonnegotiable for maintaining the high standards of patient care and safety your institution is committed to. Unless you're specific in your request, there will be confusion about what needs to be done (or not) moving forward.

Be careful when offering support. Although it's essential to be supportive, emphasize that the responsibility for improvement rests with the staff member. You should be there to assist, but the obligation is on them to enhance their image, which is crucial for maintaining the high-quality care your institution is known for. This stance prevents dependency and promotes accountability, which is crucial in the fast-paced and high-stakes health care setting.

Be prepared for pushback. In fact, anticipate it—it's a natural response. However, it's crucial to maintain your composure and keep the dialogue centered on the matter at hand.

Instead of allowing their response to sidetrack the conversation, seize it as a chance to emphasize your expectations and the importance of meeting them. Instead of leaping to defend your stance with rigidity, pause and truly hear what your staff member articulates.

Misunderstandings, fear, or frustration often underpin their responses. This attentiveness not only demonstrates respect for their viewpoint but can also diffuse tensions, paving the way for a dialogue that's both more constructive and collaborative.

While you can acknowledge their emotions as a way to navigate through their initial reactions, seize the moment to once again clarify the issue at hand, the solution you discussed, and the impact it otherwise has. By reiterating the conversation's objective—to foster their development and enhance overall outcomes—you underscore the collective aim of this exchange.

Finally, remember, your conversation is not a personal critique from you, and similarly, their reaction is not a personal attack on you.

Summarize what was discussed and announce a follow-up. As you draw the conversation to a close, it's essential to encapsulate the key points discussed. This summarization isn't just about reiterating the issues at hand but about confirming the mutual understanding and the commitment to the agreed-upon actions. It's a moment to ensure no detail is lost and both parties are aligned in their expectations and responsibilities.

Announcing a follow-up or a check-in at a specific date is the next critical step, one that underscores your dedication to the process, the individual's progress, and the overall success of your institution. However, this promise carries weight only if it's fulfilled. Failing to follow through not only diminishes the effectiveness of the initial conversation but also erodes your authority and credibility.

End the conversation on a neutral note. The way in which such a conversation concludes can significantly influence the subsequent actions and attitudes of your staff member.

It's essential to strike the right balance in the closing moments, ensuring the staff member doesn't leave feeling overly discouraged or burdened by the discussion.

Conversely, ending on an excessively optimistic note might dilute the importance of the feedback you have given, a phenomenon I refer to as the "sandwich issue": when the critical message is sandwiched between two positives, potentially lessening its impact. Aim for a neutral closure, such as "Let's go back to work," which signals the discussion is complete and is just one of many interactions you have in your leadership role.

Document the exchange. This ensures there is a clear record, safeguarding both you and your institution against future misunderstandings or disputes regarding performance or conduct.

Start by documenting who was present during the meeting, capturing the full context of the discussion. It's vital to include the date, time, and location, to anchor the conversation in a specific moment and place. This level of detail provides a foundation of transparency and accountability for all parties involved.

Next, meticulously record the substance of the meeting. What issues were discussed? This includes the initial observations that prompted the conversation, the feedback you provided, and the staff member's response.

Crucially, detail the agreed-upon actions, including who is responsible for what and the timelines for these actions. This clarity prevents any ambiguity about expectations and responsibilities, ensuring everyone is aligned on the path forward.

Furthermore, outline the expected outcomes of these actions. What changes or improvements should result from this intervention? This sets a clear benchmark for assessing progress and effectiveness. Finally, specify the follow-up steps, including who will carry them out and when.

Documenting these aspects creates a comprehensive and indisputable record of the conversation. And this thoroughness underscores the gravity with which you, as a leader, approach your role, demonstrating a commitment to fairness, transparency, and the growth of your team.

When you encounter a situation that falls outside your direct span of authority, the key is to approach it with a blend of tact, diplomacy, and strategic influence. Perhaps you're leading a project with staff members who don't directly report to you, or you're in a matrix organization in which your influence is more lateral than vertical.

In this case, it's not recommended that you have this kind of conversation. Instead, engage with the individual's direct leaders or with those who have the authority, sharing your observations and concerns. To them, position your feedback not as criticism but as an opportunity for collective improvement, emphasizing the shared mission of providing exceptional care. In these delicate scenarios, your role as a leader is to facilitate positive change indirectly, using your influence to advocate for standards and behaviors that align with the organization's values and objectives. It's a dance of diplomacy, requiring patience, empathy, and a strategic understanding of organizational dynamics.

As you can see, leadership is a journey filled with challenges and responsibilities. It demands courage to engage in difficult conversations, wisdom to navigate the limitations of your authority, and the vision to see beyond immediate issues toward the greater goal of positive change. Always remember, the true mark of leadership is not just in wielding authority but in inspiring growth, fostering resilience, and leading by example, even—and especially—when the path is complex.

Chapter 10
Moving Forward

If You Think You Can't,
Well Then You Can't.

Chapter 10: Moving Forward

As we reach the conclusion of our exploration into leadership and the art of professional identity within the health care sector, I hope it has become clear that investing in your image of leadership is not just a matter of personal pride but a strategic component of your professional development.

This investment, particularly in a field as critical and visible as health care, yields dividends far beyond the superficial, impacting patient trust, team dynamics, and career advancement. The question now is not whether you should refine your professional identity but how committed you are to the journey of continuous improvement and excellence.

In the ever-evolving landscape of health care, where challenges and opportunities coexist, the imperative to stand out for the right reasons has never been more acute. The ability to distinguish oneself through a combination of expertise, empathy, and exemplary professional conduct is what sets true leaders apart. Such leaders craft an identity that resonates with the values and missions of their institution, the expectations of their patients, and the aspirations of their team.

This book has aimed to guide you through the nuanced dance of professional identity, blending the science of first impressions with the art of a sustained imprint. From the subtle cues conveyed by attire to the profound influence of digital footprints, every aspect of your professional identity has been dissected, offering you a blueprint for intentional self-presentation.

Now, about that potato chip on the cover. Did you notice?

At first glance, it may seem like a whimsical choice for a book dedicated to such a serious topic. Yet it serves as a powerful metaphor for the concept of identity—personal and professional alike.

Imagine, for a moment, we're embarking on a journey together through a bustling supermarket. As we navigate the aisles, our attention is drawn to the myriad of products vying for our attention.

The significance of packaging design becomes strikingly apparent—the strategic placement of brands, the few critical seconds that influence our decision to add an item to our cart. It's in these moments that the familiarity of a trusted brand effortlessly convinces us to make a purchase, while the allure of a new product demands our notice through meticulously crafted packaging designed to leave a lasting first impression.

Consider, for a moment, the relationship between a product and its packaging. Although they are often perceived as separate entities, the most impactful packaging designs demonstrate that thoughtful packaging can not only complement but also enhance the product within. The packaging's shape, size, colors, and imagery are all meticulously chosen to sway your decision to buy or pass.

Now, let's pause in front of the snack aisle, and let's stare at the hundreds of chip packages in front of us. Chip packaging offers fascinating insights into successful branding. Notice how the most successful chip brands manage to communicate a clear promise: "What you see is what you get." The imagery shows perfectly shaped potato chips, which conveys the product's appeal more than any description could. It's straightforward, with no frills, showing the product in its most enticing form.

Yet there's a twist to this tale, as you know. The crumbled reality inside the bag doesn't match the perfection depicted on the outside. Despite not having a transparent section to preview the contents, we're drawn in by the promise of ideal, unbroken chips. Not just once—again and again we continue to buy them, even if we're aware of the illusion.

The lesson here is profound: a compelling external presentation can lead people to embrace you, even if the internal reality doesn't quite match up (yet). Achieving the opposite effect is significantly more challenging.

For health care leaders, the lesson of potato chip packaging is a poignant metaphor for the importance of a consistent identity. You must ensure that your external presentation—be it your appearance, behavior, communication, digital presence, or environment—showcases you in the best possible light.

Just as the chip bag's imagery promises a certain quality, health care leaders must present an identity that patients and staff can instantly trust. Although no leader is without flaws—akin to the mix of whole and broken chips—it's the strategic portrayal of your abilities and quality you should put to the forefront. After a while, just as we accept the imperfect contents of a chip bag due to our trust in the brand, so too will staff and patients accept a leader's human imperfections if they believe in the leader's dedication to their role and the well-being of their charges.

Now let's take another look at the aisle of potato chips in front of us, and let's contemplate expectations. If I were to ask you to pick a spicy flavor of these chips, you'd likely subconsciously look out for a red bag. An organic variant? Green or brown.

Our brains are wired to associate specific colors and designs with certain product attributes. This principle of expectation extends beyond the supermarket aisle to the realm of leadership. Just as we have predefined notions about product packaging, we harbor expectations about a leader's professional identity.

Despite the diversity in leadership styles and personalities, certain universal expectations persist. Much as the red packaging of spicy chips easily catches the eye of a shopper looking for a zesty snack, health care leaders who present themselves in accordance with established professional norms are readily recognized and trusted.

Yes, there's certainly room for individuality and the choice to deviate from the norm, akin to a hypothetical neon-pink potato chip bag amidst a shelf of reds and greens.

A health care leader may choose to diverge from the expected visual cues, perhaps through unique attire or an unconventional leadership style. This divergence, however, can be a double-edged sword; it might pique the curiosity of some, drawing in those intrigued by the novelty and signaling innovation or a fresh approach. But it also runs the risk of not meeting the subconscious expectations of the majority, making it harder to be immediately recognized as a leader in the health care context.

Just like the shopper who subconsciously reaches for the familiar red bag and wouldn't even know there's a pink variant, patients and their families often seek comfort in what they know and trust: traditional symbols of medical authority.

Finally, established potato chip brands are usually positioned at eye level on the shelves—easily seen, recognized, and hence chosen. Influential leaders also command a presence and often warrant higher esteem, much like brands that occupy the top shelf. In contrast, lower-shelf brands—or leaders—may work just as hard but have to strive harder to be noticed.

In the competitive health care environment, being at eye level means being at the forefront of your colleagues' and patients' minds, ready to be chosen for your visible commitment to excellence, professionalism, and care. This visibility is not just physical; it extends to the overall professional identity you build as a leader.

As you turn the final page of this journey, let the enduring lesson be the art of your professional packaging—the external representation of your internal capabilities. May the professional identity you craft serve as your steadfast ambassador, communicating competence, instilling confidence, and navigating the complexities of health care leadership with grace.

Your "packaging" is not merely an aesthetic choice; it's a strategic tool that, when aligned with your skills and vision, can weather the storms of challenge and change. Let it amplify your strengths, not overshadow them.

As you move forward, may your professional identity resonate with intention, your leadership echo with impact, and your presence be felt even in silence.

Stand out not just to be seen but to make a difference, to inspire trust, and to drive progress.

Here's to the leader in you—packaged to perfection, poised for greatness, and perpetually ready to turn challenges into opportunities.

Go forth and lead, not just with authority but with the magnetism of a well-crafted identity, one that's as compelling and multifaceted as the leader within you.

Acknowledgments

To you, the reader:

This book is a testament to your journey, your struggles, and your victories. You might have reached for this book seeking guidance, inspiration, or affirmation in your role within the health care industry. Whatever your reason, I want to acknowledge you.

Thank you for choosing a path that demands so much of your heart, body, and mind. For every patient you have comforted, for every hand you have held, for every moment you chose compassion over convenience, thank you. Your passion and commitment have not gone unnoticed. You carry with you not just the weight of responsibility but the torch of hope for so many.

I'm grateful for your unwavering ethics, your moral compass that navigates through the complexities of human health and dignity. For your determination to push the boundaries of medicine and healing, to innovate for the sake of those in your care, I'm inspired.

Thank you for treating the ill, for being the pillar of strength for those who suffer alongside them. Your ability to keep a cool head during the most challenging times is nothing short of heroic. And for your constant striving to improve an industry that stands as the bedrock of our civilization, my gratitude knows no bounds.

As you close this book, remember that the acknowledgment of your work, your dedication, and your leadership goes far beyond these pages. It's echoed in the lives you touch, the communities you heal, and the future you shape.

With respect and admiration,
Sylvie di Giusto

About the Author

International keynote speaker Sylvie di Giusto brings her expertise from a successful corporate career in Europe to every presentation. Formerly the head of a management academy and innovation hub, she developed innovative leadership programs for high-end education with unprecedented training methods. As the chief of staff for the chief human resources officer of Europe's largest tourism and retail group, Sylvie coordinated all group-wide human resources teams and activities. Prior to that, at a consultancy firm, she implemented online and in-person training and development initiatives for Fortune 100 companies.

Now, extraordinary professionals at respected organizations in the world—from American Express to American Airlines, Hilton, Nespresso, Microsoft, Prudential, and even the US Air Force—trust Sylvie to help them make the right decisions that grow their brands and bottom lines. Building on her five cornerstones of *Modern Emotional Intelligence*—visual, behavioral, verbal, digital, and social intelligence—Sylvie gives her audiences "The Power of Choice," a conscious decision-making framework that allows us to understand our perceptions, choose our behaviors, and determine our best outcomes.

Sylvie is the author of *The Image of Leadership, Discover Your Fair Advantage* and the upcoming *Make Me Feel Important*. Sylvie takes audiences on an entertaining, spectacular, and thought-provoking journey through the brain and mind and from the unconscious to the conscious—and ultimately to the heights of personal, professional, and organizational success.

For speaking engagements, contact Sylvie's wonderful team at sylviebookings@cmispeakers.com, or call +1-403-398-8488.

Perception Audit

Take the free Perception Audit and unveil the image you project to the world in just 15 minutes. Receive a personalized report that illuminates how others perceive your professional identity, and learn to align your self-view with the impression you intend to make.

Are you ready to meet the YOU that everyone else sees?

Or visit sylviedigiusto.com/audit

After you've gained the clarity you need to polish your professional identity and project the very best version of you in the workplace and beyond, let's stay connected! Follow me on social media to join the conversation about *The Image of Leadership in Health Care*.

instagram.com/sylviedigiusto
linkedin.com/in/sylviedigiusto
facebook.com/sylviedigiusto
youtube.com/c/sylviedigiusto
tiktok.com/@sylviedigiusto

Your Voice and Our Collective Reach

Books—just like you—face perception challenges.

In a world where perception is reality, nowadays the value and impact of books are often judged by the quantity and quality of their Amazon reviews. So if this book has offered new perspectives or valuable insights, please consider sharing your experience online. Your review not only helps shape the book's impact but also guides others to find the same resource you did.

Your role in this narrative could just be the beginning.

For those who have found resonance within these pages and wish to spread the wisdom within their team or organization, I offer preferred customer pricing for bulk orders. Please reach out to my wonderful team at sylviebookings@cmispeakers.com, or call +1-403-398-8488. Let's empower more leaders together.

Made in the USA
Monee, IL
06 April 2024